# THE GRAND LOUVRE

## A MUSEUM TRANSFIGURED 1981-1993

EMILE BIASINI
JEAN LEBRAT
DOMINIQUE BEZOMBES
JEAN-MICHEL VINCENT

Electa Moniteur

The authors wish to thank all those who have helped them in compiling this book, particularly by making iconographic material available.

They are especially indebted to M. Michel Laclotte, Director of the Louvre Museum, M. Pierre-Yves Ligen, President of the *établissement public du Grand Louvre,* the entire staff of the *établissement public,* and all those architects who kindly provided archival material.

They also wish to acknowledge their debt to Pierre Quoniam, their companion in the Grand Louvre undertaking. Pierre Quoniam had himself written a history of the Louvre palace and offered the authors precious advice on the subject. He was furthermore responsible for the creation of the new exhibition rooms devoted to the History of the Louvre.

His untimely death before the completion of his work came as a cruel blow. His memory will remain enshrined in the Grand Louvre to which he made such a great contribution.

*Layout: Jean-Louis Germain*
*Iconography and documentary research:*
*Catherine Mariette and Françoise Faucheux*
*Co-ordination: Guillemette Morel Journel*
*English translation:*
*Charlotte Ellis and Murray Wyllie*
*Cover photo: Alfred Wolf*

# CONTENTS

6  THE GRAND LOUVRE: ENDS AND MEANS
E. B.

46  EXTRACTS FROM THE DAILY LOG
OF A COMPLEX OPERATION
J.-M. V.

92  PLANS

100  THE ARCHITECTURAL RESPONSE
J. L.

138  THE FUTURE MUSEUM LAYOUT
D. B.

164  APPENDIX
CLIENT BODY, DESIGN TEAM
AND CONTRACTORS

*View of Saint Germain des Prés abbey and the Louvre from the south in 1410.*

## THE PALACE

The Louvre palace bears the marks of the history of France from the end of the 12th century onwards. Indeed, in the course of eight centuries, no sovereign or regime has failed to leave their imprint on it to a greater or lesser extent. By opening up the remains of the Philippe Auguste castle, the works undertaken in connection with the Grand Louvre project have made it possible to add the original feudal castle (which François I started to demolish) to the architectural evidence dating from the Renaissance – that is, Pierre Lescot's Louvre and the subsequent building campaigns.

The revelation of these three centuries of the first Louvre, for the benefit of our collective memory, thus brings together the modern history of the French state and that of the stones laid in this place in accordance with the wishes of earlier heads of state and the talent of their architects.

The first Louvre castle, which was contemporary with *Château-Gaillard*, was built *circa* 1193, to strengthen Paris's defences against the Plantagenet enemy. Its history began when Ferrand of Portugal, count of Flanders, who had been defeated at the battle of Bouvines, was locked up in its dungeon.

In turn a castle, a prison, a royal or imperial residence, the seat of academies or administrations, and a museum, the Louvre established its massive structure in the heart of Paris, which gradually grew up round it. Immense and majestic, it has become part of the capital's daily life, with its pedestrians and vehicular traffic passing across and through it.

Destiny played a role here, by preventing it from remaining the enclosed palatial complex it had become. Hardly had this objective been achieved than the Tuileries palace, which enclosed the complex to the west, was burned down by ordinary soldiers during the 1870-1871 Paris Commune.

The enclosure was shattered and, ever since, the two great wings of the Louvre have stretched out from the enclosed cour Carrée towards the setting sun, seemingly opening up Paris to her urban future by means of a clear-cut perspective. Yet although universally and unanimously admired, this perspective was not devised by anyone. It came about by pure chance.

This gives some idea of the extraordinary force generated by the first stone laid at the end of the 12th century on the right bank of the Seine by Philippe II; it became a living organism which gradually changed in form and grew, in the course of a remarkable historic continuity, to become this monumental edifice that seems never to have been completed.

If the history of the Louvre represents continuity, paradoxically it also represents discontinuity. There is continuity in an architecture achieved over several centuries and finished under Napoleon III with a pastiche of the precedent set by Lescot's Renaissance buildings. There is discontinuity in the

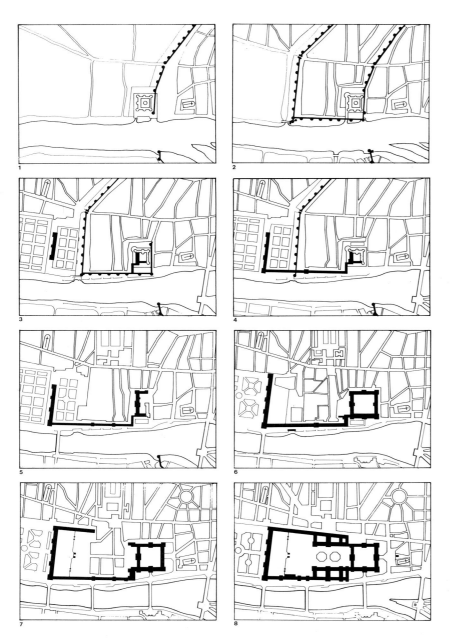

*Stages in the building of the palace:*
*1. Philippe Auguste's castle (1190)*
*The north-east section of the moat and foundations was excavated and restored in 1984.*
*2. Charles V's Louvre (1380)*
*The city wall was moved further west.*
*3. The Louvre and Tuileries palaces in 1590*
*The mediaeval keep was*
*demolished in 1528.*
*The Petite Galerie was added to the south.*
*The Tuileries palace is to the west of the city wall.*
*4. The Louvre and Tuileries palaces in 1610, linked by the Grande Galerie.*
*5. The Louvre, at the end of Louis XIII's reign (1640)*
*The enlargement of the cour Carrée has begun.*
*6. The Louvre at the end of Louis XIV's reign (1715)*
*Nothing remains of the mediaeval castle avove ground level.*
*7. The Louvre in 1848*
*The northern link between the Louvre and Tuileries palaces has been started.*
*8. The Louvre in 1886*
*Henri IV's great plan was at last complete, but the Tuileries palace was gutted by fire during the Paris Commune in 1871 and demolished in 1883.*

proliferation of different uses the Louvre was put to — uses never anticipated by those who built it, for it hardly ever served the purpose they had in mind. Several kings undertook works at the Louvre, with the intention of making it their residence. Yet over a period of seven centuries, the palace was the seat of power for less than one hundred and fifty years in all, by fits and starts, including continuous Royal occupation from the death of Henri II in 1559 until Louis XIV moved to the Tuileries palace in 1667 and subsequently left for Versailles in 1672. Those periods when the palace was put to other uses were the periods of opportunity; its vocation as a museum – or at least, its use for artistic purposes – began at the end of the 17th century, when the academies were officially installed there, the first being the Académie française in 1662. It was this vocation that was to take over in the end.

Today, the Louvre has served longer as a museum than it has as a Royal palace or seat of administration; by 1993, the collections will have been officially installed there for two hundred years. Yet the palace was never designed to house them. They were put there by the Revolutionary Convention and have remained there ever since.

The Louvre museum has never been housed in premises designed for the keeping of collections. It has had to accommodate itself to the old palace, as though a resident in an illustrious dwelling it did not choose to live in, the brilliance of which is restored by the occasional splendid evening reception but where everyday life suffers from the most uncomfortable constraints. Even if the first director, Vivant Denon, made good use of the premises and his successors have always sought to improve them, they have had "*to find space there where it could be found, to house the reserve collections, in basements, attics, dark corridors, closets, cupboards* [...] *in the countless nooks and crannies that represent an old and noble dwelling*"[1].

From the end of the 12th century onwards, the Louvre castle and then the Louvre palace never ceased to grow and transform itself. Does the name come from that of a forest where wolves *(lupus, lupara)* were hunted? Or from the term for a Norman stronghold ("lower" in Saxon)? Or, perhaps, from the romantic legend about the Belle Adeline in her *lover*'s castle? Either way, the name is now used universally.

The keep of Philippe Auguste's castle had become the symbol of the nascent French state and the anchor point of its centralised structure when, in 1528, it was pulled down, only twenty years before the first of Lescot's buildings was erected. It marked the beginning of an architectural adventure that lasted for over eight hundred years, a unique example of continuity in which the historical progress of the nation is represented in stone, in the form of the biggest palatial complex in the world.

1. G. Salles, *Au Louvre*, published Domat, Paris, 1950, p. 30.

How could so volatile and turbulent a people have succeeded in building this monument, century after century, with so homogeneous an exterior that it seems to represent a single building campaign, linking the Renaissance with the Third Republic?

Between the end of the 12th century and the end of the 19th century, twenty sovereigns and as many architects made changes to the Louvre. After Philippe Auguste who, no doubt, was personally involved with the building of the castle commanding the new Paris ramparts (sited beneath the south-west quarter of the present cour Carrée), Charles V turned the austere fortress into a Royal residence, assisted by the architect, Raymond du Temple. Thanks to the Limbourg brothers, the image of this fairy-tale castle was immortalised in the *Très riches heures du duc de Berry*, but no illustrations of the previous castle have survived. The castle was dismantled in two phases, first by François I, then successively by Louis XIII and Louis XIV, to make way for the present Louvre. Indeed, it was in 1546, a year before his death and after holding a lavish reception for the Holy Roman Emperor, Charles I of Spain, in the residence richly decorated in 1540 by Charles V (of France), that François I commissioned Pierre Lescot to build a *grand corps d'hôtel* (a large residential range) on the site of the castle. François I's son, Henri II, was to see this project to completion.

The southern and western ranges of the old castle were demolished and their substructures

*Henri IV's* grand dessein. *Fresco in the galerie des Cerfs, Fontainebleau. (c. 1600).*

*The Louvre under construction in 1650. In the foreground, the last undemolished remains of the mediaeval Louvre: the north wing of the castle and the Taillerie tower. In the background, the south-west part of the cour Carrée, built to designs by Pierre Lescot and with carvings by Jean Goujon, in the 16th century.*

used as the foundations for the new buildings. Soon afterwards, in 1563, the Queen-regent, Catherine de Medici, commissioned Philibert Delorme to build a residential palace some 600 metres to the west, on the Tuileries estate. The two palaces were sited asymmetrically, as both were aligned at right-angles to the Seine, which bends slightly at this point. The fact that the two wings later built to link the Louvre and Tuileries palaces are not parallel has posed an incessant problem of perspective since then.

When Henri IV entered Paris in 1594, neither palace had been completed. During the decade that remained to him to devote to the prosperity of the kingdom, the king drew up a *grand dessein* (great plan) for the Louvre and played a very direct personal role in its realisation. He decided to link the two palaces, to quadruple the size of what was to become the cour Carrée, and to include within the palatial complex the district which had gradually grown up between the Louvre and Tuileries palaces. In accordance with this plan, Louis Metezau and Jacques Androuet du Cerceau built the Grande Galerie, which was linked to the Petite Galerie already built by Catherine de Medici to connect the Louvre with the Charles V rampart ; this they extended beyond the city wall, to the Tuileries palace.

Just as Henri II had seen the completion the project envisaged by his father, François I, so the great plan by *Vert Galant* (Henri IV) for the Louvre

was pursued by his son and grandson. First, under the influence of Cardinal Richelieu and with Jacques Lemercier as his architect, Louis XIII added new eastern and northern ranges, completed the demolition of the feudal castle and embarked upon quadrupling the size of the cour Carrée.

Then, once Mazarin had made the necessary funds available in 1659, Louis XIV had the works continued by Le Vau. Good progress was made on site with the heightening and decoration of the Grande Galerie, the extension of the Tuileries palace and Le Brun's remodelling of the Royal apartments. But difficulties were soon to follow. The Petite Galerie was gutted by fire in 1661, and, the same year, Louis XIV commissioned Le Vau and Le Nôtre to build Versailles.

The Louvre suffered directly in consequence. Colbert, who was made *surintendant des Bâtiments* in 1664, stopped the works then in progress at the Louvre and organised a competition for the design of the prestigious facade to the Louvre opposite the church of Saint Germain l'Auxerrois. The celebrated Bernini, who had come from Rome in great pomp, was selected the architect as a result. But the matter turned out badly.

After a great number of intrigues and a certain amount of repudiation, the angry Italian departed and, in the end, it was Claude Perrault's design for a colonnade that was built.

Two major building projects represented a heavy burden on the Royal purse and the Louvre was sacrificed in favour of the works at Versailles. The Louvre was left, abandoned and incomplete, for fifty years and its state finally created a scandal. The roofs in particular had not been completed and, cheek by jowl with the Royal academies, which were the official tenants, the usable parts of the building were gradually invaded by a mob of unauthorised occupants, creating such disorder that the works had to be recommenced in 1754, first with Ange-Jacques Gabriel, then Germain Soufflot, as architect. But the works were again stopped twenty years later, so, by the time of the Revolution, Henri IV's great plan remained at a standstill.

Napoleon Bonaparte decided to relaunch it. From 1806, he put the house in order, had the squatters removed and asked Pierre Fontaine – who was to be assisted by Charles Percier – to complete the works.

At the same time, he undertook to link the Louvre and Tuileries palaces to the north, along what is now the rue de Rivoli, with a new range roughly parallel with the Seine-side wing, stretching all the way from the Tuileries palace's Marsan pavilion to the present *guichets* at the Louvre. But once again, for reasons of finance, the works had to be discontinued, both under the Restoration and under the July Monarchy.

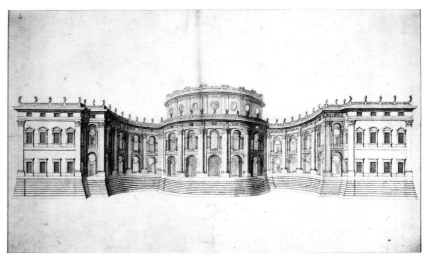

Top
*The completion
of Claude Perrault's
colonnade.
The pediment is
under construction.*

Above
*Bernini's rejected design
for the Louvre.*

11

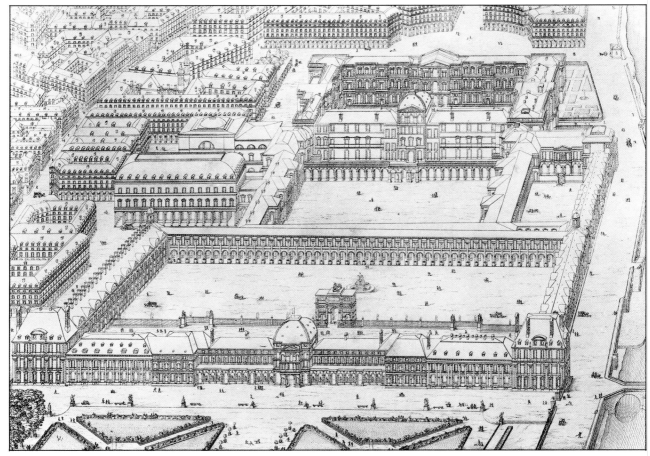

There was a new development in 1848, when the Second Republic decided to make the Louvre a "people's palace". Numerous schemes were then drawn up[2], while Felix Duban restored the facades to the southern wing (the Grande Galerie) and remodelled some interiors.

Yet while this great quadrangle of nearly ten hectares in area was being enclosed, bit by bit, the daily life of a densely populated Parisian district continued unabated at the centre, which no powers had yet succeeded in clearing. A Decree issued in 1843 was to render this possible at last, thus providing the means to complete the whole, as was to be done by Napoleon III. From the various schemes, he selected one by Ludovico Visconti (architect of Napoleon Bonaparte's tomb), which was compatible with the vast urban scheme Baron Haussmann envisaged for extending the rue de Rivoli.

Unhappily, Viconti's death in 1853 prevented the project from being undertaken as originally designed. The job was taken over by Hector Lefuel, who modified the designs and made them heavier in the process, adding overblown Renaissance-inspired ornament to the Louvre just for the sake of it and redesigning all the elevations, to give the masterpiece of 19th century French Academicism we know today. But at least he was able to complete the project and to see a Louvre palace, which was at last closed in on itself, inaugurated in great state by Napoleon III on 14 August 1857.

In fact, the works were not completed until eight years later, with the rebuilding of the western part of the Grande Galerie and the Flore pavilion. This was the apogee of the palace, the focus for high society and major official events, particularly during the universal exhibition of 1867.

The 1870 war brought the festivities to an end. The Sedan disaster and the end of the Second Empire heralded darker hours. Quite naturally, in accordance with its destiny, the Louvre could not be left out of these historic events. On 23 May 1871, three soldiers set fire to the Tuileries palace during the Paris Commune. The Tuileries palace was gutted by fire, as were the Flore and Marsan pavilions and part of the north wing, notably the library.

Lefuel restored the north and south wings to their original appearance. But the fate of the Tuileries palace provoked empassioned debate for ten years. Should it be rebuilt ? The Republic elected to do away with all the evidence it provided of past reigns, once and for all. The Tuileries palace was never rebuilt.

Paris no longer had a Tuileries palace, though even today many are still nostalgic for Catherine de Medici's "château des plaisirs" (palace of pleasures). However, in its stead, the triumphal

perspective has been opened up, from the heart of the capital, with the two great wings of the Louvre stretching out towards the setting sun, towards the splendid alignment of the Champs-Elysées and La Défense – a major axis if ever there was one and a brilliant opening marking three centuries of history, urban life and urban design, from Le Nôtre's approach to the layout of the Tuileries gardens to the present-day link between the cour Napoléon and the Grande Arche at La Défense.

For eight centuries, then, the Louvre never ceased spreading and developing[3], a giant never at rest which, in defiance of its inert stone, gradually stretched out at its own pace, in quest of a conclusive position which, until now, it seemed it should never find.

For two centuries, the museum has moved with the irreversible advance that was an integral part of 19th century cultural progress and which has reached an extraordinary rate of expansion since the last war. In the case of museums especially, this cultural progress is also connected with the formidable growth in tourism : nearly three quarters of the visitors to the Louvre today are from abroad.

Within this endlessly recommenced palace, the museum has taken on an increasingly intense, dynamic and consuming form. Sooner or later, one or other would have had to win the day: either the Louvre would have remained a palace or it would have to be entirely converted for museum use.

This two-century long, two-fold evolution had to end with the primacy of one or the other. With the Grand Louvre project, the museum has won the day – and this victory flows with the tide of history.

*The Tuileries palace fire during the Commune (May 1871). The gutted building was demolished in 1883.*

Left hand page
Top
*View of the Louvre palace from the Pont Neuf. 17th century French School (c. 1666).*

Bottom
*First Empire project, by Percier and Fontaine, to link the Louvre and the Tuileries.*

2. Over two hundred schemes for the development or remodelling of the Louvre / Tuileries complex are enumerated by the former chief architect for the palace, J.C. Daufresne, in his book *Louvre & Tuileries — Architectures de papier*, published Mardaga, Brussels & Liège, 1987.

3. This history of the Louvre palace is told brillantly by Pierre Quonian in *Le palais du Louvre*, published Nathan, Paris, 1988.

## THE MUSEUM

*The 1699 salon held in the Grande Galerie. Anonymous engraving from an almanac for the year 1700.*

The Louvre museum's official birth certificate was the Decree issued by the Revolutionary Convention on 27 July 1793, creating the Museum central des arts, to put on public show works from the Royal collections, in the Grande Galerie. The gestation of this first, official museum was a long process. Throughout the 18th century, there was very lively debate on the need to make items from the King's collection public. It was a subject on which the *Encyclopedistes* became famous, first and foremost among them Diderot, whose article on the Louvre in the *Encyclopedie* is still reknown.

The name of the Louvre already had a museum-like ring. When Louis XIV decided to abandon the palace for Versailles, the academies had been installed in the Louvre's cour Carrée ranges and in the Petite Galerie, where over four hundred items from the Royal collections were kept. Permission to visit this collection was granted fairly frequently thereafter. Exhibitions organised by the *académie de Peintures et de Sculptures* (the painting and sculpture academy), and the more or less official presence of numerous artists in the otherwise unoccupied premises, instigated the use of the Louvre as a place where the public and the collections were brought into contact. Only lack of funds prevented Louis XV from making this practice official, and, during Louis XVI 's reign, the Comte d'Angevilliers – who was *directeur général* of the *Bâtiments du Roi*, studied this possibility very seriously. The scheme would certainly have come into being, so much in favour was public opinion, had not political confusion put a stop to it. The opportunity of opening the King's collections to the public had thus been under discussion for several decades and the tide of public opinion was altogether in favour of a museum being created. Evidence of this development was supported by the fact that the study of museums was becoming a science, following the publication in 1727 of a treatise by a Hambourg merchant called Kaspar Neikal, on the best method of gathering, classifying and keeping collectors' items.

Yet the taste for collecting was far from new. Without going back as far as Egyptian funerary arrays, reference should be made to the groups of precious objects in the temples of Classical Antiquity, the *ex-voto* offerings left to be shown to pilgrims. Numerous remains survive of collections organised and negotiated by merchants in the Hellenistic era. As for the Romans, the spoils acquired by conquering armies or annexed by the governors of provinces were the object of great curiosity. And the fabrication of copies of Greek works of art gave rise to a thriving business: there are many today, in the world's major museums. A special staff, the *aeditui*, was trained under the Roman Empire, to guard this accumulated treasure. Nearer our own time, the tradition was revived by the cathedrals, whose Treasuries put the public into communion with works of art.

But it was in the 18th century that contact between the public and treasured items was to become institutionalised more or less everywhere, with varying degrees of care and know-how. This vocation, or need, came, in fact, from the wider communication of ideas and the democratizing process that was to become an imperative with the French Revolution.

This cultural explosion was no more the result of chance than was political change. It was a gradual process of crystallisation that was to result in a cultural initiative two centuries later. Everything was therefore pointing towards the Revolutionary Convention's creation of the Museum central des arts at the Louvre on 27 July 1793. The museum was inaugurated the following August. Paintings were shown in the Grande Galerie, while the ground floor of the Petite Galerie was given over to antiquities.

The new museum at once launched itself into a never-ending process of expansion. Its first director, Vivant Denon, who was appointed in 1802, began to reorganise and remodel it, most notably to deal with the extraordinary increase in acquisitions that resulted from Napoleon Bonaparte's victories. From 1803 to 1815, his museum – which became the "musée Napoléon" – undoubtedly represented the most prestigious collection of art works ever to exist. Four-fifths of them were redispersed in 1815, under the restitution imposed by the Allies.

Nevertheless, the Louvre was to develop anew, with the expansion of its collections of antiquities, resulting from the involvement of French archaeologists with digs undertaken round the Mediterranean basin. The Venus de Milo, for instance, was discovered by Dumont d'Urville and arrived at the Louvre in 1821.

To sanction this upsurge, an Egyptian department was set up in 1826, by Champollion. The proliferation and enrichment of the collections, and the activity they engendered, made daily more painfully obvious the fact that the Louvre buildings had never been built to serve as a museum. To remedy this, every opportunity was exploited, to find ever more space. The biggest of these enlargements dates from the Second Empire, when the present cour Napoléon was created by the addition of a double range to the northern wing (now still occupied by the Finance Ministry) and a corresponding range to the south, comprising the Mollien, Denon and Daru pavilions with the three associated courts known as Sphinx, Visconti and Lefuel, the last two being named after the architects who designed and saw built what was then known as the "New Louvre".

Two other major stages in the museum's gaining of the space it required were the digging of basement, in the inter-war period, to provide uninterrupted access to the four ranges of the cour Carrée at ground level; and the subsequent remodelling of the Flore wing and the Flore pavilion, which the museum had already taken over from the Finance Ministry and which were opened to the public in 1968. But by allowing the collections to spread, these works also underlined the extraordinary gigantism and diversity of the Louvre museum. In fact, seven museums are gathered together at the Louvre, under the aegis of the *Musées de France*: Painting; Sculpture; Oriental Antiquities; Egyptian Antiquities; Greek and Roman Antiquities; Art Objects and Furniture;

and Graphic Arts. Together, these constitute the biggest and most diverse assemblage in the world, in the domain of museums. The several hundreds of thousands of items represent an exceptionally varied collection and a phenomenal source of information and admiration for ever more visitors, in an old palace which is, by its very nature, inconvenient; as has already been explained, it was neither designed nor built for such a use.

The Grand Louvre project will at last make it possible for the dual nature of the Louvre, as a palace and as a museum, to be harmonized. A coherent system bringing together the various constituent parts of the palace will restore functional unity – a unity that is only apparent from outside at present. And the museum will at last be provided with the spaces it has always lacked, not only in terms of floor area but in terms of the quality appropriate to the modern services required for the collections and for the reception of the public. Until now, it has been suggested in jest that the Louvre was so poorly suited to use as a museum that one day a choice would have to be made between the collections and the public, since their combined requirements were at odds with the palace. The aim of the Grand Louvre project is to ensure the future well-being of the collections and of those having dealings with them – be it those who care for them or the much larger numbers they are intended to enrich and delight.

According to Proust, *"familiarity ends up by concealing virtually the entire universe"*. Everything seemed to have become so settled as to have given Paris her definitive form, and the

*Hubert Robert:*
*The salle des saisons*
*in the Louvre.*

Above
*Victor Duval:
View of the Louvre's
Grande Galerie in 1880.*

Right
*Hubert Robert:
Fantasy, showing
the Grande Galerie
in ruins.*

Louvre seemed to have acquired an immutable appearance. If the organic shortcomings of the museum were well-known to a few specialists, they seemed to have been virtually ordained by familiarity.

The rue de Rivoli wing of the palace stretched as far as the eye could see between the church of Saint Germain l'Auxerrois and the Tuileries gardens, in the form of a 600 metre-long barrier, preventing all north-south pedestrian movement in this part of central Paris. Who complained about the underuse

and dilapidation of the cour Carrée? Or the transformation of the cour Napoléon into a car park? Or the neglected state of the square surrounding the statue of La Fayette? And above all, who suffered most from difficulties in finding the entrance to the Louvre museum? Or the inadequacies of its facilities for the reception of the public? Or the inconveniences of its access arrangements?

Parisians had ceased using the museum, most visitors being foreigners (70%), with Americans alone being more numerous than French. Moreover, visitor totals were extremely modest for so important a cultural treasure : scarcely three million a year for a priceless collection of past riches. Was this not indeed pathetic, compared with the Eiffel tower and Beaubourg, which attracted 4.5 million and 7.2 million visitors a year respectively?

The deficiencies of this, one of our major national cultural institutions, were in any case condemned by the facts concerning its usage. For Parisians, the Louvre was certainly part of the landscape, but how many ever set foot inside ? For others, a visit to the Louvre was included among the three-star monuments without seeing which a visit to Paris would be incomplete. The proof? The average visit to the Louvre museum took one hour and twenty minutes, representing a tour at the double, through some of its galleries, in search of the best-known exhibits. The average visit lasts for three hours thirty minutes at the National Gallery, Washington or the Metropolitan, New York, which denotes the difference between fleeting acknowledgement and a life-enhancing moment of privileged enjoyment, the delight a museum should give rise to.

Talking of discomfort at the Louvre has become a truism. But visitors were not the only ones to suffer from it. The lot of those who had devoted themselves to the service of the museum was no better, far from it. There could be no better way of evoking this discomfort, and the dreams of an improvement, than to quote Georges Salles, the former eminent *directeur des Musées de France*, who described the daily problems of the Louvre museum in these words, in 1950:

*"The reserves pose us a daily problem. When the Louvre palace was made into a museum, the presentation of the collections was all that mattered. In the 19th century, a museum was no more than a stage, without what might be termed back-stage facilities. Since then, the fact such facilities need just as much, if not more, space than that front-of-house has been recognised." [...]*

*"The abundance of material in the reserves of this parallel museum should not be hidden away from people wishing to study it, or even to see it from pure curiosity. That the reserves are contained in the ancillary areas of a building which is almost entirely oriented front-of-house can be resolved only by spending a deal of money." [...]*

*"Until such expansion is allowed us, we are forced to find space where we can. [...] The picturesque is certainly winning the day as things are, and provides amateurs of the fantastic with plenty of material for their dreams. [...] But the major disadvantage of these fortuitous arrangements is that, because it is very difficult to reach the reserves, it is very difficult to move the object themselves. This hampers their examination, both by authorised visitors and by members of the technical staff, who are constantly required to refer to them, to catalogue them, to undertake studies of them, to take photographs of them, to change panel and showcase arrangements, and to oversee the comings and goings of items that are on exhibition and those that are not. Some of the former complement some of the latter, and their full importance cannot be appreciated without reference to deposits tucked away in the depths of our palace. [...] The day all the galleries and exhibition areas are open to the public, a complementary programme should be begun straight away : the back-stage facilities at the Louvre should be completely overhauled."*[4]

This first-hand account shows how much improvements of the arrangements at the Louvre represented an obvious need for all the staff. And it shows, too, how much such a project seemed purely Utopian until François Mitterrand decided to make it a reality, by taking on the patronage of the Grand Louvre project unequivocally. For it was

4. G. Salles, *Au Louvre*, op. cit.

the President of the Republic who announced, during a Press conference held on 26 September 1981, his decision that the whole of the Louvre palace should be devoted to museum use and that, accordingly, the Finance Ministry was to be transferred to new premises elsewhere.

This decision meant the Louvre palace was again to undergo major works, as was in keeping with its history. While it is true that, with the continual adaptation of rooms to meet the needs of the museum, there had never been any shortage of work at the Louvre for masons and decorators, this new project – was to, entail works comparable in extent to the most ambitious ever undertaken there. At the very least, these works would involve the complete remodelling of a truely gargantuan building complex.

An indication of its scale may be gauged from the following statistics: the perimeter totals 1 935 metres, the site covered is 51 450 m² and the useable floor area totals 145 850 m², shared between the Louvre museum (73 700 m²), the musée des Arts décoratifs (18 500 m²) and the Finance Ministry (53 650 m²).

The Louvre museum, which is the occupant of longest standing, therefore occupies the largest part. Its dynamism and natural evolution had caused it to take over more and more, over two hundred years, because of the irresistible pressure of its own life and its success.

The Grand Louvre project should represent the final step in this victorious march to its affirmation as one of the world's leading museums.

*Ange Tissier:
Plans for completing
the Louvre are shown
to Napoléon III
and Empress Eugénie
by Ludovico Visconti
in 1853.*

## THE PLANNING STAGE

Carrying out the President of the Republic's decision implied two-fold action that had, of necessity, to be coordinated : the departure of the Finance Ministry from the Louvre, and the provision of facilities necessary for the everyday existence of the Louvre museum within the palace buildings. The word "museum" implies exhibits first and foremost. It would have been one thing to augment the present museum by providing such space as could be gained for its services in the only available location, namely, by excavating beneath the courts and thereby adding to what might be termed the back-stage facilities the museum lacked. But the museum would have gained very little from such an approach – for how much space could have been gained by these means, if the original buildings were to be respected? It was quite another matter to work out the complete redeployment of all the exhibits within a homogeneously arranged palace, fully provided with the means to become a modern museum in the full sense of the term.

The selected approach was therefore based upon the complete departure of the Finance Ministry, as a necessary condition for the reorganisation of the collections.

The decision to build new premises for the Finance Ministry at Bercy having therefore been taken (the Bercy site was selected at the request of the Mayor of Paris and of the President of the Ile-de-France regional authority), work began at once.

The Grand Louvre project could thus be launched, as was done in September 1982, with the appointment of an official, to take on the preparation of the project and to run it, as two different phases:

— the first was to establish the take-over of the entire palace by the museum. It entailed both the new works required to create the new spaces and facilities indispensable to the functions appropriate to a major museum and the installation of some of the collections in the Richelieu wing on the rue de Rivoli and the associated courtyards, when these had been vacated by the Finance Ministry;

— once this phase of the take-over had been achieved, the second phase was to entail the restoration and remodelling of the historic building itself, and the reorganisation of the collections throughout the available floor area.

The first phase was thus the vehicle for the project's irreversibility. The vacation of the Richelieu wing by the Finance Ministry was scheduled for 1 January 1987, to allow an immediate start on the first phases of the works, thus facilitating an initial reorganisation of the ground floors, courtyards (which were to be excavated and glazed over) and basements directly linked with the service areas to be provided beneath the cour Napoléon.

The departure of the Finance Ministry was thus crucial to this part of the operation. Indeed, it was the basis for the whole project. Nothing more than the mere improvement of the Louvre museum's existing facilities would have been possible otherwise – and the brief for such a project would have been radically different in that case, as would have been the approach adopted by the architect.

To carry out the project as envisaged, specific legislation was required. In compliance with the Law of 1901, an Association was therefore set up on 28 October 1982, with the following members: Joseph Belmont, Emile Biasini, Guy Brajot, André Chabaud, Louis-Gabriel Clayeux, Georges Duval, Bernard Gilman, Jean-Claude Groshens, Hubert Landais, Christian Pattyn, Max Querrien, Jacques Rigaud, Pierre Soulages and François Wehrlin.

This Association for the Grand Louvre oversaw the start of the project. It was responsible for the initial decisions and the project's success depended upon the quality of its work and the realist and opportune way it put the undertaking on course; the preliminary studies, determination of the approach to be adopted, establishment of a time-table, evaluation of building envelopes, the phasing of the works, administrative organisation – all the factors that endowed the project with an efficient and rational image were due to this association. Its members were the real pioneers of the Grand Louvre project, for the *établissement public du Grand Louvre* (the public sector body set up to run the project) did not come into being until a year later, on 2 November 1983.

Its predecessor, the Association for the Grand Louvre, was provided with a budget of 1 400 000 FF by the Ministry of Culture at the end of 1982, and was thus able to start work at once.

One of its first concerns was to designate an architect capable of bringing a fresh eye to the project. Obviously, this did not mean dismissing anyone. But it seemed very clear that it was indispensable to see the project in a new light. Georges Duval, who was chief architect for the palace and therefore in charge of the building and any changes made to it, agreed to an outsider being brought in. And as it was natural such should be organised with Georges Duval's collaboration, that is what was done. Before the statutes for the future client body – the *établissement public* – could be drawn up and given official approval, to confirm what might be arranged with the participation of the future *établissement public*, the preparation and choice of who was to take on and undertake the basic architectural design had to be undertaken without delay.

The American architect, I.M. Pei, was consulted by the association, with the full approval of the President of the Republic, who wanted Pei to be appointed architect for one of his *grands projets*. Because of his past work, notably the National Gallery, Washington and the Fine Arts Museum, Boston, I.M. Pei is generally considered one of the world's leading specialists in the field of museum design. I.M. Pei was furnished with a contract as

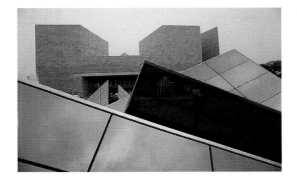

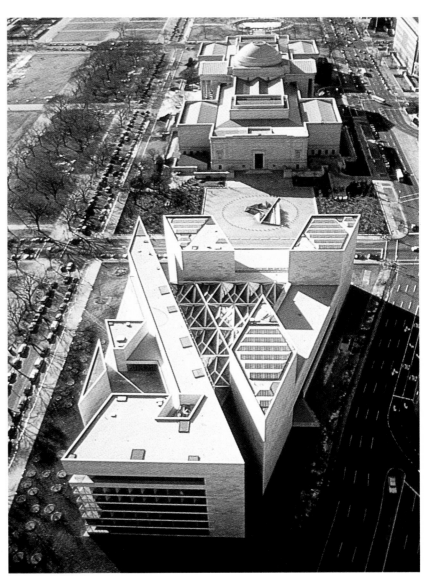

a consultant and asked to draw up a feasibility study, which was presented to the President of the Republic at the Elysée Palace in May 1983. Following this presentation, I.M. Pei was officially commissioned to undertake the design by the President of the Republic, who, moreover, assured Pei he would not be left to "depart from France like Bernini" – a reference to the misfortunes of an illustrious foreign architect in France three centuries earlier intended to reassure Pei, who had had his fingers burned when designs he had prepared for a building at Tête-Défense reached deadlock.

Ieoh Ming Pei then joined forces with Georges Duval and selected Michel Macary as his guide to the Parisian architectural world, thus providing himself with the local technical grounding and logistical means he needed. Relations between the two men were soon excellent and they formed a team to undertake the project, with I.M. Pei – the undisputed leader – making important parts of the scheme Macary's responsibility. Teams of architects set up under Pei, Duval and Macary to oversee the running of the project were to be joined later, following a competition, by the technical design offices Sogelerg and Serete, with Pei remaining in overall charge.

At the same time, a brief-writers' competition was launched; this involved inviting multidisciplinary teams to put forward proposals about the means to be adopted in the execution of the Grand Louvre project. This was not an architectural competition, as the architecture of the Grand Louvre was not at stake. It was a competition for ideas concerning the museum content of the project, and upon the remodelling to be undertaken to render it compatible with the aims of a major modern museum. Of course, this limited competition did have a bearing on architectural matters. Everyone was aware that, even if the building envelope was to be preserved at all costs and the "Royal" interiors respected, the Louvre palace must still be laid open to all the changes necessary for the future development of the museum.

The analysis of the museum's needs were set out as follows in the competition documents sent to competitors :

19

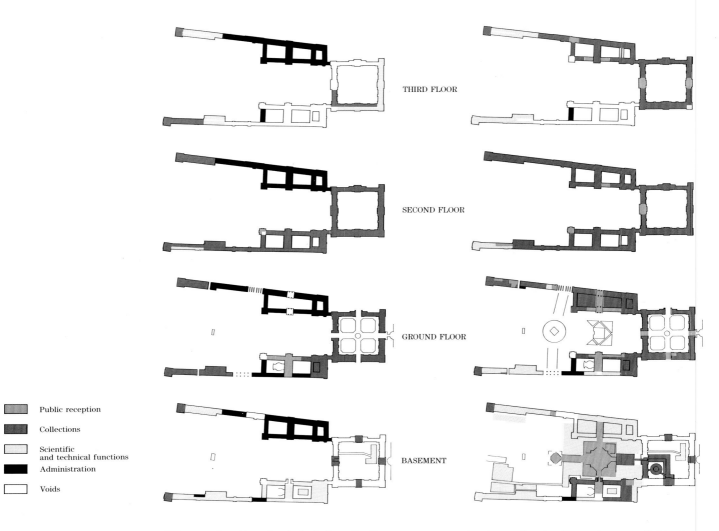

THIRD FLOOR

SECOND FLOOR

GROUND FLOOR

BASEMENT

Public reception

Collections

Scientific
and technical functions

Administration

Voids

*The changing pattern
of floor-area allocation
in the Louvre.
Left, the former layout.
Right, the new layout.
On completion of works,
the museum is to occupy
the major part of the palace.*

*"From a functional point of view, the Louvre museum and the musée des Arts décoratifs suffer from inadequacies of access which hamper the public — be it well-informed amateurs or privileged connoisseurs – from gathering in front of the art treasures. The very nature of the public has changed profoundly. Numbers have tripled in thirty years and its multiplicity has been confirmed; there are now some 3 500 000 visitors a year, including tourists from the regions and from abroad, scholars and students, researchers, art professionals and art amateurs, some in groups, others visiting the museum individually. The needs of these new visitors vary. The museum must be both a lively place of learning and a place of relaxation. This has changed the requirements for exhibitions, curatorial work and study very profoundly. New, varied and more plentiful spaces and facilities are therefore required.*

*The accommodation now available to the Louvre museum and the musée des Arts décoratifs does not meet these new requirements, either in terms of space, facilities or staff.*

*Initial analyses show the main inadequacies as being:*

*— access difficulties surrounding both museums. The entrances to these museums are not clearly apparent, because of the very nature of the palace and its evolution over the years. Visitors are often disoriented, with the Denon pavilion offering the only reference point – but even so, it does not stand out clearly, in the way it might be supposed the entrance to so prestigious a place should;*

*— inadequacies in the spaces available for receiving the public, meetings, assembly of groups, rest and relaxation, teaching activities, the reception of children, and the provision of cafeterias and restaurants;*

*— painfully inadequate internal circulation, both vertical and horizontal; complex and poorly signposted circulation routes for visitors, lacking any mechanical provision;*

*— insufficient means for protecting buildings, people and exhibits from risks of fire, theft, damage, attack, accident and variations in temperature and humidity;*

*— insufficient and inadequate space for reserve collections, workshops, storage, delivery access, offices, study spaces and lecture halls."*

This official report objectively resumes the situation suffered daily by those who had to work at the Louvre. It cannot be repeated too often how very poor their working conditions were. Apart from the premises occupied by the executive staff of the Louvre museum and the *Direction des Musées de France* on the ground floor, between the Visconti tower and the *guichets*, curatorial and administrative staff had very poorly disposed, hard-to-reach offices spilling over into every available space, despite some improvements arising from the recent creation of subterranean premises for Egyptian and Greek Antiquities. At best, they took up spaces intended for exhibits, as did the reserve collections of paintings and the conservation workshops, so preventing the major rooms round the cour Carrée from being used for exhibition purposes. The museum was not able to show everything in an area of 73 700 m², with the northern schools being particularly poorly represented : of a collection comprising 1 152 pictures, only 373 were on show. The Islamic collections remained in crates and the Art Objects and Furniture Department lacked tapestries of major importance. A complete inventory would be tedious here, but deficiencies in hygiene and security should be mentioned, to stay nothing of the effects of all these shortcomings on the running and presentation of the museum, constrained to the point of immobility by the lack of space and inconvenience, to the detriment of highly qualified but resigned curators. For all of them, the Grand Louvre project seemed to be a deliverance, and all committed themselves to it with enthusiasm.

The jury for the brief-writers' competition met on 28 and 29 April 1983 and selected a team comprising Sodeteg, with Jérôme Dourdin as consultant. Starting work immediately, in close cooperation with the architects and the museum's chief curators, they were able to prepare a document, known as the pre-brief, in the given time limit. This document was submitted to the statutory authorities at the end of 1983. From that starting point, their activities developed on two fronts, in accordance with the project's specific cost limits.

The aim of the Grand Louvre project was indeed that the Louvre museum should take over the whole palace, hence facilitating the reorganisation of the collections, while also restoring the building. But to bring about this transformation and development of the museum's content, there was an absolutely basic need to provide the future museum with the means of functioning and receiving the public it so sadly lacked. Hence, quite apart from the museum's content, there was a fundamental need to provide the museum with accommodation for reserves, workshops, offices, technical services, reception and information spaces, restaurants and cloakrooms – all commodities of which it had urgent need. Basic facilities were indispensible, as they would be for any museum, regardless of what exhibits were to be shown, just as hospitals need operating theatres, regardless of the type of surgery to be undertaken there, or kitchens are needed by restaurants, whatever type of food is to be served. It cannot be repeated often enough that the Louvre was never designed to be a museum and that is prestigious spaces were never provided with the facilities for administrative and technical back-up without which no major museum can live.

For the material benefit and security of the collections, and to enable the curatorial staff to do its work without impediments at last, it was therefore essential to inject the building with the facilities necessary for the running of the museum. Facilities for the reception of the public also implied the means for dealing with large crowds with ease. It is currently acknowledged that, like theatres, museums should be provided with as much space for their non-public activities as space open to

visitors. Yet at the Louvre, space available for back-up services represented less than 15% of the useable floor area, an imbalance that more than explained the museum's inadequacies.

The first priority of the Grand Louvre project, therefore, was that it should meet the everyday needs of the museum. Once completed, exhibition space would be increased by 80% and space for receiving the public and back-up facilities by 190%, giving a ratio between the two of 55/45, in line with current standards.

I.M. Pei's scheme represents the resolution of this need. The reorganisation of the museum's content constitutes a separate problem, to meet other needs. It will, of necessity, be undertaken at a slower pace, for it cannot be embarked upon until the physical metamorphosis has taken place, in association with the Finance Ministry's departure from the Louvre. As the former is to happen at a later stage, there is more time to prepare this element.

Its consideration was nonetheless dependent upon the location of the various departments[5] and the allocation to each of the necessary space for its expansion. Refined gradually by the chief curators, with diligent guidance from Jérôme Dourdin and continuous coordination from Pierre Quoniam, an ever increasingly precise degree of detail has been achieved by this analysis. Decisions have been reached on the future siting of the collections and on the scheduling of their phased relocation, following the completion of the works on the new accommodation, which is to be handed over to the various departments as and when it becomes available[6]. This continuous process will thus take as its first priority the technical restructuring of the Louvre. This must be undertaken ahead of the reorganisation of the museum's content, which is the ultimate goal of the operation. But the two programmes of work must necessarily be coordinated and considered together, in order to achieve greater depth, little by little, in a repetitive process with which interested parties, particularly the curatorial staff, have been constantly involved.

---

5. The increase in area for each department will be as follows :
— Egyptian Antiquities ........................ +64%
— Greek and Roman Antiquities ................ +75%
— Oriental and Islamic Antiquities ............. +55%
— Painting ................................... +53%
— Sculpture .................................. +43%
— Art Objects and Furniture .................. +57%
— Graphic Art ................................ +49%
6. The reorganisation of the museum's content is described in the fourth part of this book.

PROJET DE MONUMENT
A LA GLOIRE
DE LA RÉVOLUTION FRANÇAISE
VUE PERSPECTIVE

*Louis Ernest Lheureux: project of 1889 for a monument in the cour du Carroussel, to commemorate the French Revolution.*

Right hand page
Top
*I.M. Pei designed the pyramid to create a sense of spaciousness in the naturally lit new entrance beneath the cour Napoléon.*

Bottom
*The museum has been housed in the southern part of the palace since 1793. It was arranged in a linear manner. The Finance Ministry formed a barrier to the north. The Grand Louvre project entails the reorganisation of the museum's collections in the ranges round the new entrance in the cour Napoléon. By this means, the museum will become more compact and walking distances will be much reduced.*

## THE APPROACH

The first phase of the works, known as the I.M. Pei phase, which is the physical manifestation of this brief for organic change, thus represents a profound morphological transformation of the Louvre palace. The museum currently occupies the southern part of the palace, where it is housed in accommodation disposed in the shape on an 'L', with the Perrault colonnade forming the foot of the 'L' and the Seine-side galleries the stem, terminating with the Flore pavilion.

When the Finance Ministry has left the Louvre, the museum will take the same form as the palace itself, which could be described as a 'U'. As the historic buildings are protected by law and do not always lend themselves to the installation of modern facilities on a scale that would be inappropriate to rooms of inflexible form, the only way to create new adaptable spaces was to excavate in the middle of the 'U', thus turning the museum into a compact quadrangle.

In this new form, it is to be arranged around a central focal point, with multidirectional routes leading from it. Such is the function of the new entrance foyer – the great turntable located in the centre of the cour Napoléon, in the middle of the 'U', signalled at ground level by the pyramid.

Obviously, from this central point, distances will be reduced. At present, Michelangelo's Slaves (in the basement of the Flore pavilion) are 800 metres away from the Winged Bulls of Khorsabad (to the

north-east of the cour Carrée). This distance will be three times less when the Slaves are relocated in the galerie Mollien and the Winged Bulls in the cour de la Poste. The central entrance beneath the pyramid will mean the furthest department will be less than 200 metres from the starting point of the visit.

This radical transformation of the museum's use will have no visible effect on the palace externally ; its appearance will be carefully preserved, while invisible cross-links are created below ground level, to give direct and convenient routes between its parts.

I.M. Pei had completed his preliminary design work at the end of 1983 and official approval could therefore be sought through the proper administrative channels, and was to be obtained early in 1984. Having first been presented to the President of the Republic, the file was submitted to the *commission nationale supérieure des Monuments historiques* on 23 January 1984, which gave approval after a very lively sitting. The proposals were then literally demolished during a seminar held outside Paris and attended by everyone with a direct role to play in the undertaking : chief curators, administrators, architects, engineers and brief-writers.

Thus for three days, about one hundred specialists were able to pick the proposals apart and make all the necessary analyses and corrections. At the end of this meeting, the Louvre's chief curators took the entirely spontaneous and unprecedented

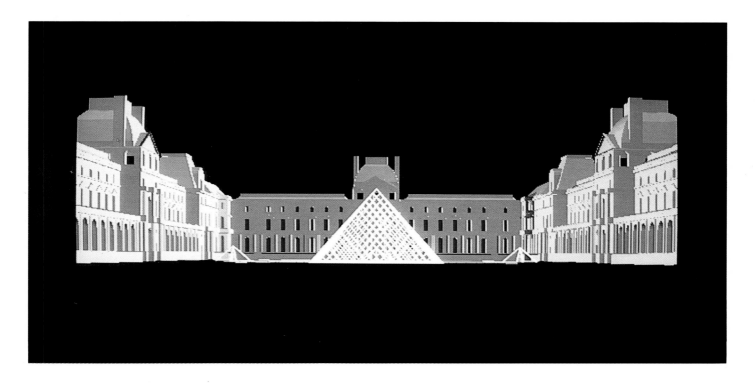

step of publishing a statement, confirming that they fully supported I.M. Pei's project and were in favour of its being executed:

*"All the problems posed by the execution of the 'Grand Louvre' were investigated during a three-day seminar at Arcachon, attended by the various authorities concerned :* the établissement public du Grand Louvre *set up to build the project, the* Direction des musées de France *executive, the Louvre museum executive and curators, teams of architects and brief-writers.*

*The seminar was the outcome of a prolonged period of preparatory work, begun in April 1982 and followed up on a regular basis from June 1983 onwards. This provided the brief-writers with the means of getting to know the needs, goals and tendancies of all the interested departments and services.*

*It was therefore possible to propose an overall brief and to discuss and perfect it, both in terms of the future use to be made of the wing of the Louvre to be vacated by the Finance Ministry, and in terms of improving the museum's existing spaces, to give a satisfactory allocation for the collections held by the Louvre museum's seven departments in the building as a whole. Indeed, it was no longer appropriate to see the Finance Ministry wing simply as an extension to the present museum, and miss this very exceptional opportunity to revise visitor routes round the museum by including the vast numbers of exhibits of every kind which, owing to lack of space, are now in the reserves, and to*

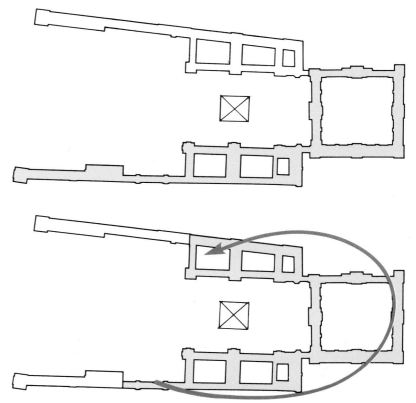

"*The pyramid can only be justified and explained as the emerging part of an underground architecture that has been inspired by the indispensible alteration – for museological purposes – of the morphology of the Louvre palace. It constitutes the ultimate visible gesture of a "buried architecture"; like the dome of a building it is subject to an irrefutable internal logic: that of transforming the two wings of the Louvre palace into a compact ensemble and providing the palace with the reception, technical, management and scientific facilities that are sorely lacking.*"

Presentation of the project by I.M.Pei to the *commission supérieure des Monuments historiques.*

*Once I.M. Pei had determined the project must emerge above ground level, he decided upon the pyramid. In his submission to the commission supérieure des Monuments historiques, he refuted the alternative possibilities of a dome, a cube or a smaller pyramid.*

*improve upon the currently very poor reception and visitor facilities.*

*It was in accordance with these aims that certain principles were agreed upon: a single reception zone, to be located as centrally as possible; the reorganisation of exhibition spaces round the cour Napoléon, thus keeping linear extension of the museum to a minimum; and the development of service spaces, both for the public and as required for the running of the museum.*

*As agreed unanimously by all participants, the brief as a whole is notable for its concern to open up the museum to the public while retaining all the traditional pedestrian routes, including the passage Richelieu — the architectural quality of which is frequently overlooked because of its relatively inaccessible position in the midst of the Finance Ministry. Visitor routes within the museum are envisaged which are more logical, interlinked wherever possible to provide chronological or historic coherence. These routes will be well provided with rest areas and information points.*

*The unceasing concern of all concerned with the brief was to create 'the world's greatest museum' without giving way to gigantism of the kind that would make the whole into an unvisitable monster.*

*In the context of the Grand Louvre project, it appeared to the chief curators in charge of the various departments that I.M. Pei's pyramid was the symbol of the entrance to the museum. Far from being the 'modernist gimmickry' or 'gratuitous architectural gesture' it has sometimes been dubbed, it is, in fact, a proposal which –*

*though perhaps daring – forms an integral part of an overall architectural scheme that is unanimously appreciated and accepted for its coherence and quality.*"[7]

The motivation behind the issuing of this statement was the subject of much speculation. There were those who were determined to see it as the result of shady or underhand dealings, no doubt because they were unfavourably disposed towards the scheme. Yet nothing could have been clearer or more straightforward. Shocked by the unyeilding, biased hostility expressed by some, and realising the Grand Louvre project could provide the solution to problems that had so long beset them, the chief curators wanted to make a public declaration of their support for a scheme which they were convinced would benefit the Louvre and which they dreaded might collapse under attacks from detractors who included some eminent people but were for the most part badly informed. The chief curators' support has never waivered since that moment. It was absolutely crucial to the success of the undertaking, because it expressed the commitment of those most concerned.

7. The statement was published in the Press on 3 February 1984; the signatories were: D. Alcouffe, Chief curator, Department of Art Objects & Furniture; P. Amiet, Chief curator, Department of Oriental Antiquities; R. Bacou, Chief curator, Department of Graphic Art; J.-L. de Cenival, Chief curator, Department of Egyptian Antiquities; J.-R. Gaborit, Chief curator, Department of Sculpture; M. Laclotte, Chief curator, Department of Painting; and A. Pasquier, Chief curator, Department of Greek and Roman Antiquities.

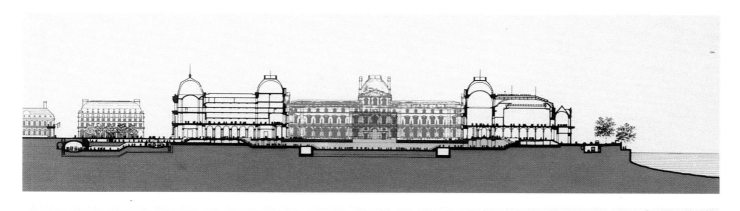

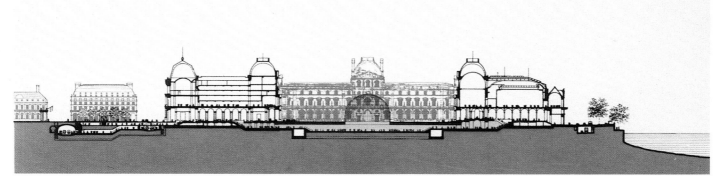

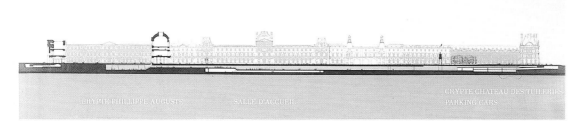

CRYPTE PHILLIPPE AUGUSTE      SALLE D'ACCUEIL      CRYPTE CHATEAU DES TUILERIES
PARKING CARS

*Preliminary proposals*
*for the cour Napoléon:*
*A cube*
*A dome*
*No structure*
*above ground level*
*Pyramid with 30° slope*
*Pyramid with 45° slope.*

9 . 3 5 m

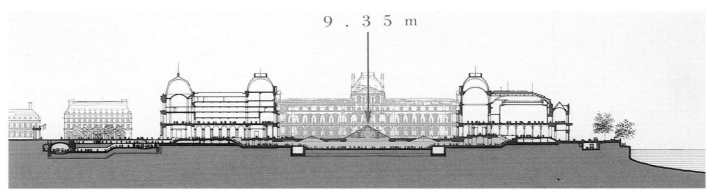

1 6 . 2 m

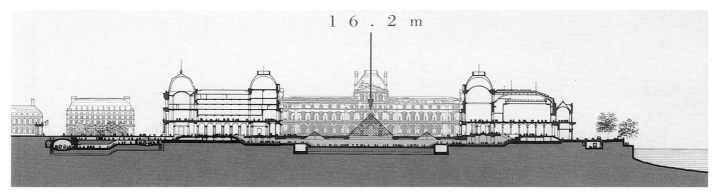

## THE PYRAMID

From the start, the Grand Louvre project was the subject of discussions with the Mayor of Paris, who took a very close interest in it and never failed to support the project, despite considerable reservations expressed by his entourage. These good relation between the City of Paris authorities and the *établissement public du Grand Louvre* were largely responsible for the very close cooperation between officers and technicians throughout the undertaking on such statutory matters as the rerouting of public highways, public safety and building regulations approvals, adequate provision of public utilities (gas, electricity, sewerage, etc.), and consent for collaboration between the *établissement public* and the Semah (the body in which the City of Paris had a majority interest, responsible for running the Les Halles project) that led to considerable savings in air-conditioning plant being achieved, and so on. The interest Jacques Chirac showed in the Grand Louvre project, in his capacity as Mayor of Paris, and his favourable opinion of its architectural form – including the pyramid – was particularly valuable when public debate erupted on the publication of the first images of its external appearance.

The photograph of the pyramid published on the front page of *France-Soir* on 24 January 1984 gave rise to a real explosion, the first step in one of those battles Paris delights in. Response in all the media was immediate, as much because of the Louvre's world-wide reknown as through the international repute of the architect, I.M. Pei

Debate was lively, with each camp taking up its position on the basis of a political quarrel, as was reflected journalistically. The France of the Right and the France of the Left confronted one another in a dispute which, absurdly, even extended as far as archaeology, drawing distinctions between ''Right-wing archaeology'' and ''Left-wing archaeology'', on the basis of insinuations made about the two teams of different origins undertaking digs, one in the cour Carrée and the other in the cour Napoléon. ''A megalomaniac and disastrous scheme'', ''bomb crater'', ''fit only for Disneyland'', ''the Luna park of the Louvre'', ''the house of the dead'' are a few of the names plucked at random that the pyramid's detractors dreamed up to describe the project.

Controversy continued throughout 1984, the picturesque and ever-more vocal parade being brought to a halt only with the erection of a full-size simulation of the pyramid, at the request of the Mayor of Paris, during the 1985 May Day holidays. It was an immediate popular success. But above all, it provided visitors with the means to appreciate the exact size of the ''object'', which became better known to everybody. The public realised it was not going to be a gigantic appendage, blocking views of the Louvre. After that, the project's future irreversibility seemed assured. Archaeological digs were then reaching completion and construction work was in the throes of being started on site.

But the artificially stormy and public aspect of this dispute should not be allowed to cloud the real issues : the very nature of the Louvre museum, its vast size and the layout of its entrances.

Reference to the distances to be covered by visitors inside the Louvre museum well conveys a basic problem, that of the Louvre's very organisation as a museum.

Many wondered why the Grand Louvre project did not take the opportunity to rid the Louvre of the gigantism resulting from the accumulation there of seven separate museums, which are known as Departments ! It was rightly pointed out that such vast conglomerations are no longer in fashion and present-day taste is for smaller museums on a more human scale. As Paul Valéry once put it, ''*I do not like museums much; many are admirable but none are delicious*''. The Grand Louvre project would thus run counter to the trend towards intimate museums with a human face. This is certainly true. The Louvre is famous for its universal, historic character and is among one of the very few museums, like the Prado, the Metropolitan and, above all, the Hermitage, to exhibit such multiplicity and variety.

The choice here is a matter of policy. Not having decided to give up the Louvre in order to build seven smaller museums elsewhere (and such a decision would have been highly questionable, for the Louvre museum's multidisciplinary character could be said to benefit each of its parts) the very nature of the museum had to be accepted and the most made of it. Yet the contents could not simply be redistributed at will; heavy items (antiquities and sculpture) had to be at ground level, while paintings needed to be naturally lit, from above, and hence could be located only where rooflights could be provided. Art objects came between the two. As a result, extensive use had to be devised for each level, but the building could not be sliced up vertically, like a cake : such problems are inherent to a museum housed in a palace that was never designed for such a purpose.

The word ''Louvre'' conjures up the wonders of Paris in the world's imagination, with the museum and palace mixed together. It did not seem appropriate to separate these two elements. Yet once the decision had been taken to retain this combination, the inadequacies of the existing arrangements had to be remedied and the palace converted to a museum use not envisaged by those who had built it.

The Louvre's vast size is among its defects. It will be overcome by the compact form the future complex is to take and the considerable reductions in walking distances that will result.

When the Grand Louvre project is completed, visitors will no longer have endless inconvenient distances to walk. Both horizontal and vertical circulation routes have been carefully worked out, with special attention paid to disabled people who, until now, have been very poorly catered for at the Louvre. The Grand Louvre project envisages their access more or less everywhere. As to those already familiar with the Louvre museum, who want to find and enjoy a favourite work of art, the new arrangements will mean they will never be far away from it. They, too, will benefit from the reductions in distances, the improved routes, presentation and quality of services in a museum they can continue to frequent. If they really enjoy the Louvre as it now is, their pleasure should be in no way diminished in a Grand Louvre designed for the comfort of all.

Another basic objection concerns the main entrance beneath the pyramid which detractors insist upon describing as the only entrance.

It should first be pointed out that this will not be the only entrance to the museum. Other entrances will be retained at the Louvre, for all those who know the museum or who use a particular service, so giving direct access to specific parts of the building. But it is true that the cour Napoléon entrance (beneath the pyramid) will be the only entrance to be fully provided with the reception facilities and services designed to meet visitors' expectations. Such an arrangement is in keeping with the museum's usage (how many major public buildings, particularly museums, are organised round several entrances?) and with good management (running costs should not be overlooked).

The new visitor reception area will be accessible by three different routes, which means visitors will assemble in the entire area lit by the pyramid – over 2 000 m² – where visitor movement has been calculated on the basis of a notional peak-period maximum of 5 000 people at a time. Saturation would be reached above that figure, when waiting would become a necessity[8].

Located at the centre of the building, the new main entrance allows for an increase in capacity and for reductions in with the excessive walking distances the Louvre now suffers from. But the objections raised by the project's detractors to a single entrance would seem to be a red herring, a smokescreen raised by those unwilling to countenance the pyramid.

Let us now discuss the pyramid, starting with its architecture.

It was originally agreed that the building of anything above ground level should be avoided, at all costs. In the course of his design investigations, I.M. Pei nevertheless felt the need to make his "buried architecture" communicate directly with the outside world, for two reasons. First, the need for volume and light; second, vertical communication in the relationship between the old and new buildings – a concern that ruled out excessively

<hr>

8. If this maximum were maintained constantly, the total number of visitors to the Louvre would be 24 millions a year.

24 January 1984.
*The Louvre project*
*is the front page story*
*in* France-Soir.
*The controversy begins.*

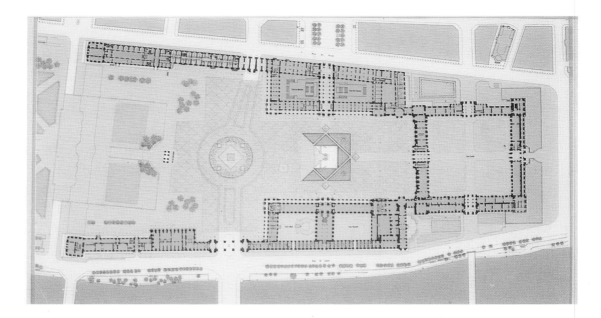

*Plans
(ground floor,
mezzanine,
and reception)
of the detailed design
submitted by I.M. Pei
in January 1984.
The principles governing
this project
were accepted.*

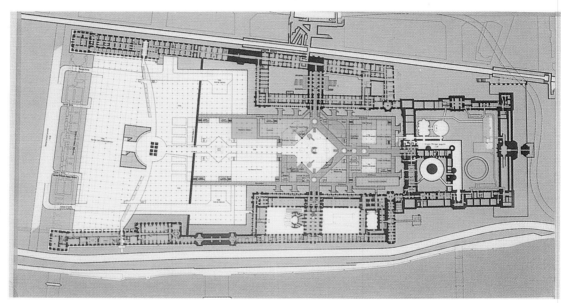

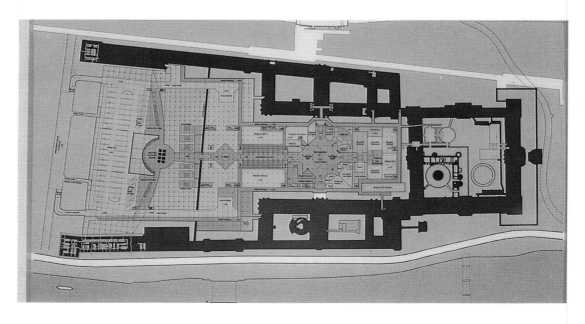

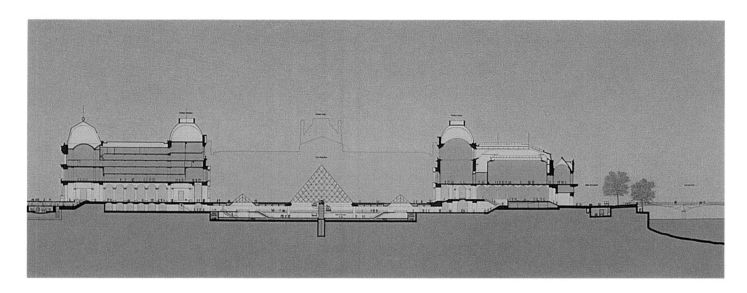

deep excavation for the new visitor reception area. Nine metres seemed a reasonable depth to Pei, partly because of the Seine water-level, but also to avoid a subterranean sensation being created by too great a rise in level between the new visitor reception area and the rest of the museum. He feared low ceilings would create an oppressive atmosphere unworthy of the Louvre, and that this could not be overcome by the provision of a flat glazed ceiling at ground level, as this would give a dull light. Hence although the architect embarked upon his initial design investigations with the intention of respecting the original requirement of not building anything above ground level, he gradually sensed the need to establish a more comfortable relationship with the exterior and suggested a big enough volume might be created to prevent the new visitor reception area from resembling a metro station. Of course, he needed daylight in any case. Lastly, and still more important, he wanted to retain visual contact between visitors and the palace.

All underground architecture creates a sense of disorientation. I.M. Pei wanted to be sure visitors would never forget the Louvre palace and that they would remain aware of its architecture. The entire system of visitor directions has been worked out on the basis of topographical consciousness, as rendered permanently legible by the pyramid.

I.M. Pei gained approval for a device to emerge from the new visitor reception area at the end of that spring. He chose the pyramid at the beginning of that winter, after investigating other forms – domes, cubes and so on. The pyramid was chosen because it took up the least space, provided the best upward views from the bottom of the new visitor reception area (which, of course, were oblique), and, lastly, because its layout was similar to the gardens designed by Le Nôtre for Louis XIV at the foot of the Tuileries palace – gardens which Pei

suggested might be reinstated, to replace what is now known as the "*jardin réservé*" (which date from the reign of Louis Philippe). Pei's design for the pools round the pyramid is based directly on Le Nôtre's garden layout. These pools, which add an extra element of elegance, cover exactly the same area as the new visitor reception facilities and hence reproduce their form at ground level. Pei's whole project abounds with extremely refined details of this kind, representing what almost amounts to a language in code, for architectural enthusiasts. Far from being the strange, impertinent object its detractors saw it as being, the pyramid was born of the architect's respect for the Louvre palace and his desire to prevent anyone from forgetting that, when entering the new underground visitor reception area, they were also entering the palace, and history too. It could therefore be said, without the least paradox, that the pyramid represents a homage to the Louvre.

Once these major matters had been agreed, the scheme had to be worked out in detail and preparation made for the start on site. Time was at a premium here, too.

While the architects, engineers and technical design offices prepared tender documents and setting out drawings, the archaeologists took over the site and the restoration of the cour Carrée was begun, under the supervison of Georges Duval.

*Detailed design: cross section. January 1984.*

*In 1984,*
*an exhibition was held*
*in the Orangerie,*
*in the Tuileries gardens,*
*and the first scale model*
*of the project*
*was put on public display.*

30

## UPS AND DOWNS

The archaeological digs represented the project's kick-off on site, for they were the first works to be undertaken, as a mandatory preliminary to the construction works. As the cour Napoléon constituted a part of central Paris until the 19th century, traces of urban life were harboured underground there. These had to be recorded and drawn up, as a statutory condition, before they could be destroyed – provided no unexpected treasures were discovered. The only such discovery (made by the contractors) was the counterscarp wall built to designs by Le Vau in Louis XIV's reign, in front of the Sully pavilion. This surprised everyone. Its importance and quality were deemed worthy of preservation. Measured drawings were therefore made of this wall, which was then taken down, integrated into I.M. Pei's plans (which involved a certain amount of amendments), then rebuilt, as the approach to the remains of Philippe Auguste's castle. The overall cost of this 'surprise' was eighty million francs.

To meet the schedule, site preparation was begun, tender documents were finalised and tenders were invited at the same time.

Whereas the archaeological digs in the cour Napoléon were a statutory condition of the works, those conducted in the cour Carrée had a more particular purpose. In accordance with a proposal made by Michel Fleury (supervising archaeologist) and supported by the great historian Georges Duby, this special undertaking was included within the scope of the Grand Louvre project. Georges Duval (chief architect for the Louvre palace) was put in charge of the works and the restoration of the cour Carrée was begun at the same time as the archaeological dig. The archaeological works as whole were put under the control of a commission, and Georges Duby agreed to be its president, assisted by Paul-Marie Duval (an expert in mediaeval archaeology). This commission, which consisted of eminent historians and archaeologists, met frequently and provided valuable support for the project's good progress, by tempering relations between the *établissement public du Grand Louvre* and those in charge of the site. The Grand Louvre project thus embraced the entire history of the Louvre, with Philippe Auguste's keep – the symbol of the Capetian origins of the French State, representing the mediaeval beginnings of an architectural journey which has the pyramid as its modern ending.

The restoration of the cour Carrée represented the real beginning of this archaeological work. The first sod was turned on 15 March 1984. Despite the tight schedule given them, the archaeologists rose to the occasion and handed over the site to the contractors as planned ; the contractors also had a tight schedule to meet.

The works proceeded apace, under the efficient guidance of Jean Lebrat (manager of the *établisse-ment public du Grand Louvre*), in spite of all the difficulties posed by the different origins of the teams involved, the participation of partners not particularly familiar with this type of work, the constraints arising from the very nature of the Louvre palace (an historic building requiring a high degree of protection), the shortage of technical information about it, and the continued day-to-day existence within it of the museum and the Finance Ministry, at such close proximity to the site.

But far greater difficulties were to come, with the changes made to the schedule which followed the legislative elections in the spring of 1986.

Until then, the project had enjoyed a particularly privileged position, thanks to the close personal interest of the President of the Republic, which had meant all problems had been resolved. This position was reversed after the change of government, and the masterplan was subjected to continual erosion for two years.

At the end of the period known as "political cohabitation", it might be said that, if the Finance Ministry had not won entirely, the Grand Louvre project had not entirely lost. But the project had been demoted to the status of a run-of-the-mill affair. Its principal purpose was denied by the Finance Ministry's continued presence in the rue de Rivoli wing, and it was condemned to follow the normal procedures for public works projects, with only ordinary budget allocations. Such a fate was in keeping with the Louvre's history of sudden boosts and moments of brilliance, followed by sudden collapse and prolonged periods of stagnation. Even though the then Culture Minister, François Léotard, supported the project, the *établissement public du Grand Louvre* was forced to make cutbacks and to compromise with its opponents by May 1988. The project had certainly reached an irreversible stage, both in fact and, moreover, in public opinion. But its completion receded into an uncertain, distant future as ill-defined, unwieldy arrangements blurred the horizon.

In essence, the project was intended radically to transform the shape of the museum, rendering it more compact by organising the exhibition spaces round three sides of the new, central main entrance beneath the cour Napoléon. But once the vacation of the rue de Rivoli wing had been blocked, at least in part, by the Finance Ministry's reluctance to move out, all reorganisation of the museum became impossible or was considerably slowed down. I.M. Pei well described the situation when he said that, without the north (rue de Rivoli) wing, the Grand Louvre project was like a man with an amputated arm. Such certainly seemed to be the fate in store for the Grand Louvre project when the relocation of the Finance Ministry was called into question between April 1986 and May 1988, while Jacques Chirac was Prime Minister.

Although I.M. Pei's architectural approach was never challenged officially, it was effectively betrayed in these new circumstances. The initial

desire to undertake the project as quickly as possible, so that it became irreversible at the very least, was entirely vindicated. The original schedule envisaged that the Finance Ministry would have wholly departed from the Louvre by the end of 1986. An immediate start on works to the Richelieu range (on the rue de Rivoli) was to have followed the first phase comprising underground links with the new visitor reception area beneath the cour Napoléon, the glazing over of the three courtyards and the installation within them at ground level of Sculpture and Oriental Antiquities (the Chevaux de Marly in the cour du Ministre and the Assyrian Bulls in the cour de la Poste), with the remodelling of the rest of the building forming part of a second phase of works. The arcade known as the passage Richelieu in the middle of the range bounded by the rue de Rivoli was to be opened to the public, so linking the place du Palais-Royal and the Palais-Royal métro station with the cour Napoléon, by means of a pedestrian "umbilical cord".

The passage Richelieu would thus have provided pedestrians with a direct means of access to the cour Napoléon, past exhibits which would have been visible to the public through glass. This urban entrance to the Louvre in the heart of Paris would certainly have contributed a major link between the city and the museum and was among the strong points of I.M. Pei's design. But it could not be carried out without the departure of the Finance Ministry.

As the Finance Ministry's departure had been called into question and largely rescheduled, weeks of discussion were necessary to reach agreement on how works might proceed, at least on works indispensable to the functioning of the new visitor reception area: provision for service runs from Les Halles via the cour de l'Oratoire, the installation of a main security point at ground level in the first *guichet*, the construction of ventilation shafts in the courtyards and the opening up of the passage Richelieu to the public.

Agreement was reached in July 1986 and works could be continued, subject to costly and time-consuming conditions, including the construction of a sound baffle and to the works being undertaken only at night. The preliminary part of the programme was thus achieved, albeit in a form reduced to the bear minimum.

Nor were site works interrupted while negotiations continued on the vacation of the Finance Ministry premises at the Louvre. An official decision was reached in July 1987 : the Finance Ministry would vacate the Louvre — but it would now do so in two phases. The two courtyards to the east of the passage Richelieu would be handed over at the beginning of 1989, when the work of covering them over and installing within them at ground level works from the collections would become possible. Yet without contesting that the Finance Ministry would leave eventually, it was decided the Finance Minister and a staff deemed indispensable to him would remain at the Louvre for an indefinite period, in premises above and to the west of the passage Richelieu, round the courtyard known as the cour du Ministre and in the Rohan range, until such time as the problem of their relocation was resolved – to somewhere other than the purpose-built new Finance Ministry offices at Bercy.

What remained of the Grand Louvre project?

That it would be completed one way or another was obvious, because of the strength of its architectural logic, its logic for the museum and the natural force of the trend that had made it a necessity in the first place, then subsequently rendered it irreversible. But it was another matter to see the project through within a specified time limit, with the concentration of resources and will-power required for so out-of-the-ordinary project which, as it were, constituted an affair of state. And it was another matter, too, to bring such an undertaking to its conclusion, by way of the daily agendas of administrative concerns and a series of annual budget allocations that would inevitably be called into question constantly, unless it were given the priority which alone could guarentee exceptional impetus.

The Grand Louvre project was still a major project, but it had to compete with so many other initiatives, all of which needed funds; so many other undertakings which had to be seen through! A ten-year programme had been duely drawn up in mid-1987 and, having received the approval of the then Culture Minister, François Léotard, it had been passed to the Finance Ministry at the end of the same year. It was to have served as a basis for discussions and for working out budget allocations. But part of the money already allocated had been frozen, design work had been held up or stopped and the preliminary development of the museum had been slowed down.

How long would it take to complete this adventure, now it had become locked into the daily grind? There was much food for pessimism in a strangely similar precedent. After the Tuileries palace had been gutted by fire (see p. 13), the Third Republic decided, on 26 June 1983, that the Finance Ministry should be concentrated in the Louvre's rue de Rivoli wing and that the Flore pavilion, which it had occupied until then, should be given over to the Louvre museum. This decision was duely put into effect – but the Finance Ministry did not vacate the Flore pavilion until 7 November 1961. Once the necessary works had been carried out, the museum's new accommodation there was inaugurated by André Malraux (the then Culture Minister), on 2 April 1968. The affair had dragged on for seventy five years!

How long was this ultimate take-over of the Louvre by the museum going to take?

If public opinion was not up in arms, it had begun to mock the stubbornness of the Finance Minister. An *association des amis du Grand Louvre* (Friends of the Grand Louvre) was set up in July 1987, with the aim of defending the project by all possible means. Its president, Paul Delouvrier, wrote to the candidates in the second round of the 1988 presidential elections, asking them to state their position on the Grand Louvre project.

François Mitterrand replied that he had *"not taken the decision to undertake the Grand Louvre project in order to leave it a building site"*.

He was re-elected President of the Republic on 8 May 1988 and the Grand Louvre was to become a reality. Michel Laclotte has the task of making this reality live. Having been made the first director of the Louvre museum by devolved statute, he at last has the necessary administrative powers for this task, over and above his personal influence and experience, gained in organizing the Orsay museum. He heads a team of curators who have devoted themselves unstintingly to the success of the Grand Louvre project. The entire future of this great adventure lies with him: it is in good hands.

*I.M. Pei and François Mitterrand with Jean Lebrat and Emile Biasini beneath the Richelieu pavilion during a site visit in Spring 1987.*

If one looks at the Grand Louvre today for the first time, the immediate impression is that no other architectural approach could have possibly provided the new museum spaces that were so vital and, at the same time, have preserved the historic integrity of the existing fabric.

I.M. Pei has created modern underground spaces in which visitors are constantly aware of the presence of the Louvre palace above. Consummate professional skill has translated an architectural challenge into a demonstration of the obvious.

The clarity and purity of the forms that he has expressed – using such contemporary materials as glass, steel, stone, and white concrete – highlight the majestic palatial environment. The result is elegant harmony.

It is, however, a well-know fact that nothing in the world is more difficult to achieve than simplicity.

In the same way that nature hides infinite complexity beneath the outward beauty of the body, I.M. Pei had to conceal the intricate networks – vital to the functioning of the building – behind each ceiling unit, deep inside each structural post.

Countless hours of research, calculation, discussion and argument lay behind the achievement of such purity. Although any construction project of such magnitude inevitably involves such factors, in this case the proximity of the venerable palace, the historic nature of the site, and the sheer number of participants involved in the project amplified the entire process. How was one to react when the bulldozers uncovered a 17th century counterscarp wall standing in the middle of what was planned to become a space for lively activities? Or when the planned internal service route ran into the Charles V rampart? Or when one of Bernard Palissy's kilns suddenly emerged in the middle of the laboratory delivery area?

Page after page would be required to tell the full story of the everday vicissitudes experienced by the team responsible for the project. Moreover, their attempts to overcome seemingly impossible odds were complicated by the added constraint of a tight schedule. Although their efforts were crowned with success they will always remember the Grand Louvre project as an unforgettable challenge in their professional careers. Never had such simplicity been achieved at such painstaking cost.

One of the team kept a detailed log of the entire proceedings. Before going on to describe the overall project in detail we have felt it instructive to present a few extracts from his account of the daily adventure that it involved.

## EXTRACTS FROM THE DAILY LOG OF A COMPLEX OPERATION

*The cour Napoléon.*
*Spring 1984.*

*Visitors can just
get round the entire Louvre,
inside and outside,
in the course of
a whole afternoon's walk.
The palace is not
exactly in line with
the monumental east-west
axis of the capital.*

## JANUARY 1984

On the second, the president of the *établissement public du Grand Louvre* assembled his full team: fifteen people in all. The first operational members had just arrived.

The newcomers – accommodated in cramped, temporary premises in Rue Notre Dame des Victoires, where they had to cross the director's office to reach their own cubbyholes – knew little for certain other than that they were all there to design and build the Grand Louvre.

But what was the Grand Louvre, other than a powerful concept? At that stage it implied no more than a dream – materialized by a dozen plans for a project which, four years later, would involve tens of thousands of plans.

At first sight, the most striking feature was the simplicity and straightforwardness of the architectural scheme. An entrance under the pyramid led to a naturally-lit reception area nine meters further down, from whence the visitor went up to a mezzanine, affording entrance to the three main buildings of the future museum: the Denon pavilion, the cour Carrée, and the Richelieu pavilion.

Visitors would have an uninterrupted view of the palace; at all stages natural lighting shone down, or beckoned them on.

At that stage of development, the concept was clear enough to feature the essential, yet still hazy enough to rule out objections of a secondary nature.

Thus, the program itself was little more than a preliminary program: a series of charts and figures showing eventual floor areas, along with draft outlines of the functions and the inter-relationships of the spaces, illustrated by two diagrammatic plans showing the locations of the major functions.

It was necessary to ascertain whether the challenge raised had at least met with an architectural response befitting the Louvre; in an unusual move, Ieoh Ming Pei had therefore been asked to submit a first preliminary design scheme as early as Spring 1983.

On 23 January, the *commission des Monuments historiques* approved I.M. Pei's preliminary scheme; finally, on 27 and 28 January, the future users of the museum, in turn, gave their approval. By early January 1984, the project was ready to get underway.

All the operational tasks lay ahead: the program, budget, planning, design contracts, archaeological excavations, survey of the existing structures, test borings, design and works; not to mention the setting up and organizing of the client bodies who would be responsible for planning, allocating, coordinating, supervising and paying for the work of the hundreds of contractors who would execute the project.

### The lie of the land

The first task was to identify, as far as possible, the major constraints which all those involved would

invariably be confronted with at each stage of an exceptionally lengthy project.

The whole process would extend over some fifteen years: basically, once the reception area in the cour Napoléon had been completed, the redeployment of the collections – in successive "instalments" – would take at least ten years. The museum had to continue functioning; the alternative would be to close it for several years, during which time the public would have no chance to see the masterpieces it housed. This was out of the question, as was closure of the Ministry of Finance. In concrete terms therefore, ways would have to be contrived of keeping open the various entrances to the museum, of re-routing service networks such as telephone and power lines without dislocating them, and of ensuring fire safety (by maintaining access for fire services etc.) The list of potential problems was endless.

– Large scale urbanism was a central feature of the project, owing to the central Parisian location, and because of the extent of the areas to be built or redesigned. The component elements of the project not only varied, they were furthermore staggered over time; thus, it was not possible to define each stage of the design process with the same precision. Accordingly, the ground to be covered was mapped out, ranging from the most straightforward – and soonest to be completed – tasks, to those which were least well defined. This allowed design work to proceed, but also meant that a careful eye

Above
1865: The new Louvre
is completed
and Henri IV's grand project
is finally realized.
For a further six years
the cour du Carrousel
would form
the main courtyard
of the Tuileries palace.
The first French railway
was only thirty years old.
It would be another
thirty five years
before the first metro line
was opened.

Opposite
A century later,
the Tuileries palace
has gone.
The population of Paris
and the Greater Paris region
has risen from two
to ten million inhabitants.
Hundreds of cars are parked
in the cour Napoléon.

*The statue of Lafayette – still brandishing his sword – is finally removed from its plinth.*

calculated, however, it would become a constraint. Assessing the feasibility of what would become a firm commitment therefore implied an all-round approach involving several independently conducted investigations in order to minimize the risks of error. Later, it would be necessary to provide the personnel and set up the appropriate legal machinery in order to supervise costs and to ensure that they were respected.

– The site – the *domaine national du Louvre et des Tuileries* – had a long history. No alterations could be carried out without consulting the numerous individuals and bodies who had partial or overall responsibility for the prestigious patrimony, nor without their prior agreement being obtained. These included the Head Architect of the Louvre, the *commission des Monuments historiques*, the *commission des Sites*, and the *association de défense des Tuileries*.

– Finally, in order to establish the irrevocable nature and the very credibility of the project, the first phase had to be completed swiftly. Regrettably or not, the age of the great cathedral builders had vanished – times had changed, and organization, means and methods all had to follow suit. Given the deadline for completion, an initial choice had to be made as to how to apportion the available time between the main phases of development.

## The time schedule

Starting with the final objective and working backwards in time, the major interlinking phases could be briefly described thus: building works followed on from design work; in turn, the designers – the architects and engineers – could not proceed until they were in possession of a program, a survey of given factors concerning the site, and a contract.

The initial schedule for the cour Napoléon allowed for six months to draw up a contract and a program, and to assess the givens, followed by eighteen months of design work and two years of building works. Then came the schedules for the cour Carrée – a mere eighteen months for design and building works, and for the Richelieu wing – eighteen months of works once the Ministry of Finance moved out of the building. Given the available time, this was the best possible allocation and the choice was butressed by the constraint imposed by the archaeological excavations: one year for the cour Carrée, two for the cour Napoléon. The entire process could be smoothly integrated providing the archaeological excavations began the following month. The Ministry of Finance, however, was to be evacuated in two stages: early July 1986 for the ground floor and courtyards; early January 1987 for the other floors. This meant eighteen months in all, with the added constraint of continued functioning – a constraint which proved virtually impossible to meet. One had only to imagine for an instant six months of building works going on on the the ground floor and a Ministerial Department functioning on the floor above.

had to be kept on overall coherence and balance between the works to be provided at each of the stages defined within the long process. And there was a further difficulty: much of the new layout was to be underground.

Archaeological excavations had to be completed before any works could be undertaken. In the case of the cour Carrée, the aim was to highlight Philippe Auguste's fortified castle; and even in the cour Napoléon, where routine urban archaeological excavations were scheduled, there was always the slight risk that – despite the odds – some unexpected vestiges might have to be preserved. This could - at the very least – jeopardize the time limit, or the coherence of the project. Although excavations carried out by Berty in the nineteenth century provided a fair estimate of what lay beneath the cour Carrée, the sole evidence in the case of the cour Napoléon came from a few dubious plans. What might remain of this part of Paris which had been ploughed up by contractors in the previous century to extract building stone as if from some rich mine seam?

– Although the Louvre was a magnificent palace, archival material was sketchy; there was a conspicuous lack of information concerning the level of the foundations, or the various service systems which had been installed over a century ago, or the condition of the floors.

– Moreover, it was necessary to provide a cost estimate for the first phase of the project and, at that stage, costs could only be assessed by summary investigation. Once the cost ceiling had been

## FEBRUARY 1984

### The Louvre turned upside down

However, no matter which area was concerned – cour Carrée, cour Napoléon, or Richelieu wing – or which constraints involved, the first challenge was to draw up a program, an inventory of givens, and a contract within six months, always providing that the archaeological excavations also began in the following weeks.

At that point, in early February 1984, archaeological excavation meant that the areas where digging was to take place would first of all have to be cleared of any obstacles. Although the cour Carrée was clear, the Cour Napoléon was one vast parking lot, with the Ministry of Finance car-park on the north side, and the museum and the *Direction des musées de France* car-parks to the south. Two squares, planted with hundred-year-old trees, were surrounded by a sea of automobiles. In the middle of each square stood a statue. The statue of Lafayette – triumphantly brandishing his sword – remained a problem. It stood in the epicentre of the Louvre, and an equally symbolic site would have to be found; furthermore, the consent of the

National Daughters of the American Revolution would have to be forthcoming.

A site on the cours la Reine, near the bridge, was mooted. It was an ideal location for the statue, but might not the brandished sword – now pointing East – give rise to a diplomatic incident? And if it were installed on the other side of the street, might it not seem to be pointing aggressively West? While such matters were being debated, the statue

Above
*Archaeological excavations,*
*uprooted trees,*
*and dismantled statues:*
*the journey to the center*
*of the cour Napoléon*
*has begun.*

Opposite
*A tub to fit*
*the hundred-year-old tree;*
*a tank transporter*
*was needed*
*to ship it off.*

Opposite
*1830: the palace forms
an almost entirely
enclosed compound.
The urban fabric
is steadily retreating
and city houses
occupy only a few
remaining plots.*

Below
*In the 16th century,
the Tuileries château
was built in what was then
the outer suburbs.
The tile kilns
can still be seen
buried under the site.*

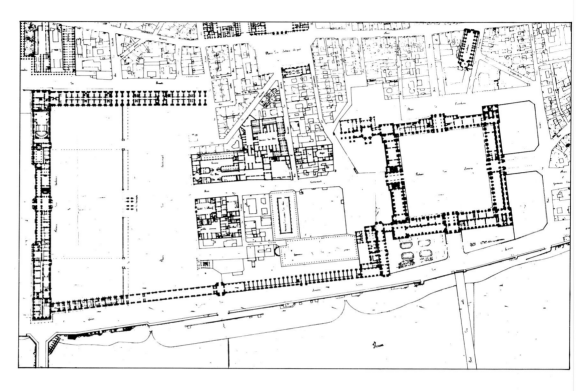

could always be removed from its plinth and kept in the square.

For the hundred-year-old trees the alternative was straightforward: they could either be felled or transplanted ; after all, apart from some of the smaller ones, most of them were only some twenty to thirty meters high. Normally, three years were required for the safe transplantation of such venerable flora, to allow for gradual pruning. Only two short months remained before 31 March 1984, after which date it would be necessary to wait until mid-November when the sap would begin to once more recede. In this case, the *établissement public de la Villette* was called in: the future park at La Villette could provide a new home for the trees. La Villette would also field the skilled expert needed to carry out such a lightning operation. Although the expert in question reckoned that only one in three of the trees would survive, the experiment nevertheless went ahead.

There was still the problem of the automobiles. After due consultation, the Ministry of Finance agreed to remove some of them pending alternative solutions to be found for the remaining vehicles. This dragged on because, although the solution was at hand – neighbouring public car-parks were in deficit through lack of customers – no budgetary provision had been made for such expenditure. The only condition laid down regarding the partial evacuation of the ministry car-park was that the museum, in turn, remove its own vehicles. The museum retaliated, laying down a reciprocal stipulation.

And then, there were also the archaeologists. They too needed to organize themselves, to hire personnel, to program their work, and so on. The excavation costs were included in the project budget; an agreement would have to be drawn up with the *Association française pour l'archéologie nationale*. The exceptional time limit called for exceptional means: in two years, a hundred archaeologists were about to undertake a program which, in normal circumstances, would have taken ten archaeologists over twenty years; extra labour would be required to shift and dispose of the 60 000 m³ of earth to be excavated. The tendering included a contract for large-scale earthworks to go below the three-meter deep geological soil level, down "into the mists of time". For the project was to go deeper – just how deep, no one at that point knew. Excavations were to begin at the eastern end, in the cour Napoléon, where there were neither trees, statue, nor too many vehicles.

### The survey

Although the program only remained to be drawn up (the preliminary program having been completed), the inventory of technical givens, on the other hand, had to be begun from scratch. There were neither surveyors plans, nor geohydrological data, nor any plans of the hundred-year-old underground networks.

Opposite
*A page from a book*
*than only a few can decipher.*
*The archaeologists*
*revealed a veritable slice*
*of the underlying strata.*

Below
*The excavation site*
*is starting to resemble*
*a vegetable garden*
*in which only the gardeners*
*dare to venture*
*off the planked pathways.*

54

## The plans

The surveyors plans – on a scale of 1/200 for the exterior (44 hectares), and 1/50 for the interior (15 hectares), along with some sections – would provide a sufficiently accurate picture of the building: Tendering procedure had to be drawn up within six months; a surveyor would have to be consulted, officially appointed, and commissioned to draw up plans. In this case, an outside expert was called in – the official surveyor employed by the *établissement public d'aménagement de la ville nouvelle de Cergy Pontoise.*

The exterior of the buildings formed the framework within which the project would be inserted, and full measured drawings were required, including the streets around the palace.

On the other hand, the interior plans could not all be drawn up at once. Only the areas corresponding to the first phase of the project were of immediate concern, and could be actually surveyed within the deadline. As this basically involved the Ministry of Finance offices, lengthy negotiations were instigated.

## Water

Among the natural elements involved, the river Seine – flowing in the immediate vicinity – was of prime importance. Here as elsewhere, the water table rose and fell with variations in the river level. The Technical Director of the Louvre could not recall the palace basements having been flooded by the rising waters in the course of his thirty five years of professional experience.

But how much lower than the basement level could one go? The riverside motorway on one bank, and the Metro line on the other, provided initial guidelines; for further details, the *Bureau de recherche géologique et minière* (Geological and Mining Research Office) was called in. The Brgm had carried out a technical survey for the nearby Les Halles project, and was responsible for monitoring variations in the Paris water table. At the same time, the Brgm was asked to conduct a geological survey. The upper level of the limestone layer was a vital parameter: if it were too low, foundation works would prove costly; if it were too high, then excavation work would be necessary – this would prove equally costly and, furthermore, vibration might prove damaging both to the palace structure, and to the collections such as the reserves of Greco-Roman Antiquities stored under the south-east corner of the cour Napoléon.

In order to assess such problems, sample borings would have to be made, and seepage piezometers would need to be installed to measure the way in which the water pressure-head varied with the changing level of the Seine.
Furthermore, since the works would considerably modify the hydraulic flow of the water table, a mathematical computer simulation would be required.

A safety threshold would have to be fixed. The project provided for two reserve storerooms in the cour Napoléon – one for pictures, plus an additional storeroom for Greco-Roman Antiquities. Car-parks might conceivably be flooded in the event of a full spate of the Seine, but this was out of the question where artworks were concerned. Therefore, the security threshold adopted was that which corresponded to the level of the hundred years' flood (the maximum level statistically probable over a one-hundred-year period); above this level, the floodwaters would overspill directly onto the embankments and, in such an event, there would be time to safely evacuate the artworks given the gradual rise in the water level. Below this level, and within the hypothetical threshold, the level of the water table in the cour Napoléon would need to be monitored, as would the discharge of water to the

*Historical memory stops at the foot of the well; beyond lies geological deep time.*

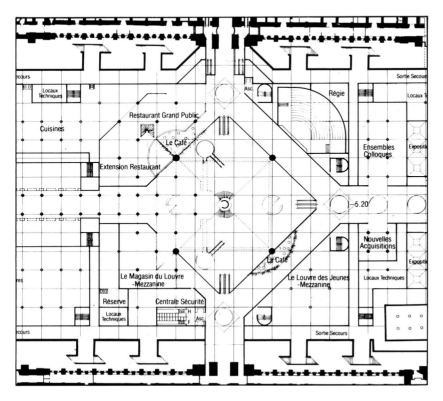

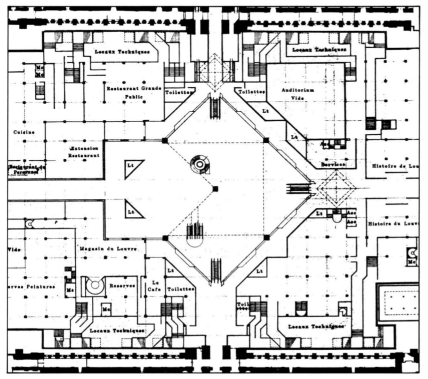

bottom of the cut, at least while works were in progress.

Where did the limestone start? To what level did the water table rise? The answers to such questions would in turn determine the level of the Napoleon reception area. The box which was to contain this reception area could in fact only be protected from seepage in two ways. The first method would involve sealing it off like the hull of a ship; the ship in question, however, was 100 m wide and 200 m long. The hull would have to be heavily re-inforced to withstand water pressure; although not impossible, this would prove costly. Nor would this prove sufficient, technically speaking. The weight of the structure would have to be increased, or the structure itself would have to be rivetted to the limestone so that the hull would not float with variations in the water level.

The second method consisted in removing the water! A permeable – rather than a sealed – hull would be built. In this way, the water would seep down and could be pumped off, thus removing the pressure and the need to re-inforce or add weight to the structure. Although earth pressure would still pose an inevitable problem, this was a more economical solution, providing the volume of water to be pumped off was not too great. The palace foundations in fact lay on subsoil which was permeated by the water table. If the flow created by pumping was too great, this would wash away the finer particles of the subsoil; in time, gaps would form, the soil would shift, and cracks would appear in the palace structure. The amount of flow would depend on the permeability of the adjacent soils (although these could be injected to make them less permeable), and on the depth under the normal water table level to which excavation works would extend.

### The underground networks

After the surveyors' plans, and the geological and geohydrological surveys, there remained another factor which had to be accounted for before design work could begin: the exact location of the networks which ran under the site and supplied the palace.

At first sight, the solution was straightforward: the various systems were functioning and all that was required was to ask whoever was running them for the necessary details. Things, however, were not quite so simple. Depending upon the type of system – ranging from sewage pipes to pressurized steam conduits – a varying degree of supervision was carried out by a dozen departments. Over the years, structures had become redundant or had been altered or re-located, whereas reliable plans covering such alterations had not always been drawn up.

One document was particularly revealing: the formal agreement setting out the respective rights and responsibilities of the State and Municipal Authorities, as regards the *domaine national du Louvre et des Tuileries*. The agreement described

in painstaking detail the number of gaslamps, how long these should be lit, and how the running costs should be shared out. It dated back to 1910. Additional clauses had been appended in the 1930s, but since then the agreement had been tacitly renewed every five years with no allowance being made for changed circumstances.

The reasons for this cautious approach were clearly formulated in the preamble to the agreement: *"The committee met several times and decided that the best course of action was to abide by the spirit which had informed the works upon which it was called to deliberate. Subsequently, on the one hand it refrained from addressing the delicate questions of ownership raised in the case of certain of the areas under consideration; on the other hand, basing its rulings upon a de facto state of affairs which it merely acknowledged, it apportioned the costs to be borne by each of the future contracting parties on the basis of whether the case involved: spaces open to the public at certain times only; spaces permanently open, but infrequently used; or, thirdly, spaces permanently open to the public and classifiable as major urban thoroughfares."*

Two world-wars later, the document was still mouldering in the Ministry of Culture files, along with two corresponding plans – equally well thumbed and tattered – in the files the Paris Municipal Lighting Department.

The competition for the program design was won by a team composed of J. Dourdin Consultants – a programing firm, and Sodeteg – a technical design office. Sodeteg were already generally familiar with the palace – they were ideally qualified to track down the right information, and to assess the reliability of such information. They were commissioned to draw up site plans on a 1/200 scale. The surveyor would then add to these plans the various features which had been accurately located – e. g. accessible sewers.

In mid-March, it became apparent in the course of design work on the pyramid – for which I.M. Pei was responsible – that simulated wind effect tests would have to be carried out in a wind tunnel, and the *Centre scientifique et technique du bâtiment,* based in Nantes, was called in.

*The archaeologists have gone; the box is ready to be built.*

Left hand page
*16 April 1984* (top)
*In the definitive sketch, the mezzanine space beneath the pyramid is symmetrical but cluttered with posts.*

*28 November 1984* (bottom)
*In the modified preliminary project, the posts have disappeared (see p. 73).*

## MARCH 1984

### The contract

Among the tasks scheduled to be carried out before early July 1984, the engineering contract remained to be drawn up. This would provide a vital blueprint for the four subsequent years.

Indeed, although the contract only legally bound the client body and the designer, its terms would be instrumental in setting the mould for the whole project; these terms would obviously govern the overall organization, the specific roles and tasks of the participants – client body, architects, construction managers and contractors – as well as their inter-relationship, and the ground rules governing such inter-relationships.

They would involve decisions concerning the fundamental options in the project. Three teams of architects and two technical design offices would be required to execute the project successfully. Given the distinctive nature of the site, no competition had been launched for the choice of architect. Several months of consultation and architectural

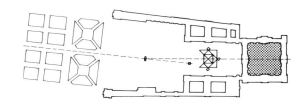

reflection would be necessary to draft a satisfactory project.

I.M. Pei was therefore approached and asked to submit a preliminary sketch – most of the personalities consulted had recommended him on the basis of his work at the National Gallery in Washington. Pei was formally appointed on 13 May 1983 by the President of the Republic. He was thus given a full mandate and responsibility for the overall co-ordination of design and works; specifically, he would be in charge of the design of the cour Napoléon.

Because he was an American citizen, I.M. Pei took on a French associate, M. Macary, whose specific task would be to design the Richelieu wing.

Because the palace was an historic monument, I.M. Pei also worked in collaboration with the Head Palace Architect, G. Duval who, in any case was officially due to restore the façades and roofs of the cour Carrée. Under the terms of the engineering contract, G. Duval would be in charge of enhancing Philippe Auguste's fortified castle under the cour Carrée, and of providing links between the cour Napoléon and the existing museum, to the right of the Sully and Denon pavilions.

Although there had been specific reasons for not launching an architectural competition, such was not the case where the choice of technical design offices was concerned. A dozen or so Parisian design offices were capable of providing solutions to the technical problems raised by the architectural design and the palace itself.

A competition would have to be launched; this would involve eight design offices, working in pairs (so that, should one office drop out, it could be speedily replaced by the other).

The proposed contract was due to feature in the tendering documents, and as two months were required to consult, scrutinize, choose and negociate, less than two months remained to draw up such a contract and to include it ready for tendering. In other words, hardly any time at all, if everything was to be started from scratch.

Of all the contracts drawn up for other major projects, the contract for the Ministry of Finance at Bercy was the most comprehensive: it would serve as a model. Given the high standard of the parties involved, this contract had obviously been the outome of carefully conducted negociations and was thus naturally commendable to the future design team at the Louvre. Administratively, it could only provide a general guideline. It was therefore adopted as the firm basis upon which to hone the specific features pertaining to the Louvre project.

## Managing the unpredictable

Generally speaking, an engineering contract includes a program which has to be completed within a given deadline, and for a fixed cost.

The specification of the program to be completed does not merely consist in enclosing the

*The walls of the moats in protective winter wrapping.*

Left hand page
*Cour Carrée
Summer 1984* (top page)
*Works in progress
on the ground level,
façades and roofs
in the world's most
magnificent construction
site.*

*Fall 1984* (bottom page)
*The original fortress
re-emerges:
the Philippe Auguste keep,
the group of Charles V
buildings, and
the François I pavingwork.*

*Cour Carrée, Summer 1985*
Top
*1.8 meter-wide scaffolding*
*enables the sculptors*
*to work at ease.*

Bottom
*At ground level,*
*works have begun*
*on the deck*
*covering the moats.*

draft of the program along with the contract. The limits of the program must also be set out.

The visitors reception under the cour Napoléon was the center of the future museum. From there, the palace could be entered from three directions: to the south, via the existing museum; to the east, via the fortified castle and the cour Carrée; to the north, via the re-arranged Ministry of Finance. These three entrances from the reception area formed the hub of the new layout. They would have to be completed simultaneously, as would the opening of the Richelieu arcade which was to run between the place du Palais-Royal and the cour Napoléon, and would provide the major link between the museum and the city.

The first two entrances did not raise any particular problems. For budgetary reasons, in the third case, only the excavation and covering of the courtyards – along with the basement and ground floor layout of the area henceforth designated as the Richelieu wing – would be completed.

Under the place du Carrousel, design work had barely started on the parallel scheme for the provision of a car-park, tour bus park, and arcade. Uncertainty reigned.

Here, however, the state budget for the Grand Louvre project would cover a part of the program which was vital to the opening of the cour Napoléon. This involved the conversion of the avenue du Général-Lemonnier into an underpass, and the provision of new laboratory facilities for the *Direction des musées de France,* along with two delivery areas where artworks and goods could be loaded onto electric-powered trucks for conveyance to the cour Napoléon and the area above it. These works were vital to the functioning of the cour Napoléon, and had to be completed at the same time as the latter. Design and construction, however, would require less time to complete and this offered some breathing space. Everything was relative!

Moreover, under the terms of the contract, design work on this section of the program – along with the layout of the upper area – would proceed with a view to overall coherence, but only up until the completion of the preliminary scheme because, at that stage there would still remain too many uncertain factors; money could not be spent, nor could detailed design work proceed were there any likelihood that the scheme might have to be entirely reconsidered.

That was not the only uncertain factor. In the cour Napoléon, both the conservation of the artworks and the provision of an underground visitor reception area meant that temperature and humidity levels would have to be controlled. In other words, air-conditioning would have to be installed. Depending upon the season, air-conditioning involved the provision of heat, or of cold, or of both simultaneously. In this case, the problem was how to provide an economical supply of cold air. Either an ice water production facility could be built in

60

*Cour Carrée*
Top and bottom right
*The painstaking work
on the roofing lead.
Even though visitors
are 45 m below,
the lead decoration
has been restored
down to the finest detail.*

Bottom left
*The eroded stonework
has been partly or fully
replaced by
new blocks sculpted
in situ.*

*Cour Napoléon*
*In March 1985,*
*when drilling began for*
*the* berlinoise *retaining wall*
*at the foot*
*of the Sully pavilion,*
*a 1.5 m-wide wall –*
*the remains of*
*an uncompleted project*
*by Le Vau –*
*was discovered;*
*(see p. 69).*

the *domaine du Louvre et des Tuileries*, or, alternatively, use could be made of the nearby Les Halles facility (a few hundred meters distant) with its available production capacity. The eventual choice called for a feasibility, nuisance and cost analysis or, in other words, preliminary design work upon which ulterior options might depend.

Concerning the cour Napoléon, the cour Carrée, and the initial phase of the Richelieu wing, the uncertainty factor was of a different nature. The furnishings program had not been drawn up: the contract contained no provision for appropriate design work.

A similar problem arose concerning the automatic telephone switchboard and the computer facilities. The necessary telephone installations – unlike the computer facilities – could be specified in a straightforward way; both factors, however, were inter-related and, given the speed of technological change, it was urgent to bide time whenever it was feasible to do so. The centralized system of technical information processing required to run the building would quite obviously be related to actual design work on the building; this system alone, therefore, was included in the contract.

### The time factor

Once the actual extent of the design process had been defined, it remained to work out arrangements whereby the constraint imposed by the time limit might be alleviated.

In any event, tendering out of separate contracts would obviously have to be launched in three main phases, beginning with works on the fabric, to be followed by the various technical facilities (air-conditioning, electrical installation etc.) and then the finishing works (flooring, facing and ceiling works). There could be no question of a general

contractor being in a position to act as a screen between the designer and sub-contractors. Moreover, such phasing would give the architects and engineers more time to study the last group of bids in detail.

The other arrangement adopted consisted in giving the designer partial responsibility for drawing up the detailed technical specifications and construcion drawings required for the immediate launching of siteworks.

A considerable time would elapse between the launching of the tenders for works on the fabric, and the actual signing of the contract, if only due to the lengthy administrative procedure involved. Advantage could therefore be taken of this interval to work up the drawings to be used on the site; in turn, this would allow for a fuller description of the works and thus – theoretically at least – a more viable assessment of the tendering price.

Moreover, when siteworks began, it would be necessary to set up a central steering unit to supervise the overall coherence of the working drawings submitted by each contractor. One can imagine the scale of the problem – seven hectares of concrete were to be poured on three different levels, and this would involve some ten thousand working drawings. Moreover, the works out to tender were staggered over a considerable period of time and not all the contractors had been appointed when concrete pouring began. Hence the reason why, at that initial stage of the contract, the designer – in the absence of any alternative party – would have to act as substitute for those contractors not yet appointed.

### The cost factor

An engineering contract also includes fees and estimates; taken together these make up the target cost: the amount which the client will have to pay for the project he intends to undertake.

The cost of works cannot be accurately assessed until design work is completed; the target cost is therefore only a provisional figure, subject to a fairly large differential. At a later stage – once detailed design work has been completed – a definitive estimate can be submitted, entailing a correspondingly tighter cost differential. Should the final cost exceed – or fall short of – this estimated figure, the designer's fees would be reduced accordingly.

The engineering contract drawn up for the Ministry of Finance Bercy project featured an additional provision – stipulating a financial ceiling which the client would not exceed – and this provision was to be adopted at the Grand Louvre. The procedure was as follows: the initial, provisional estimate for works would represent 92% of the ceiling price; the definitive estimate – drawn up once the detailed design work had been completed – along with the cost of the contactors' bids (allowing for a 3-5% increase depending upon the contract) should together come to less than 95% of the

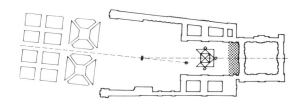

ceiling price; the final cost of works, on completion, should still come to less than 100% of the ceiling price. If such cost limits were exceeded before tenders were let, then the designer would be required to redesign the scheme at his own expense in order to meet the fixed cost envelope. In the course of works, the client could ask that the scheme be thus redesigned if this were deemed advisable. Naturally, the entire procedure was based upon the assumption that there would be no fundamental modification to the program.

The reason for fixing this financial ceiling was straightforward enough: the total cost of works amounted to almost one billion francs. Whereas adherence to the target cost proved an *a posteriori* incentive, the need to comply with a fixed cost ceiling meant that necessary adjustments could be made in the course of the design process – in other words, while there was still time to act. Indeed, the intrinsic force of inertia associated with a billion-franc project was such that any cost fluctuation would have to remedied as rapidly as possible.

At that stage of drawing up the contract, it was impossible to assess the designer's fees and the cost of works with any accuracy. The amount of fees to be paid to the technical design office would be established by the competition result; the architects, on the other hand, were asked to submit an estimate.

Meanwhile, three separate cost analyses of the project were undertaken. The first of these was carried out by the technical design office which was part of the project team and was obviously familiar with the program and the site; the second was conducted by the *société d'aménagement des Halles*, (Semah) which had experience of underground projects accessible to the general public; the third analysis was carried out by the client body which had access to details of the costs involved in other major projects.

One night in late March 1984, the hundred-year-old trees – their roots carefully protected in four-meter diameter containers – left the cour Napoléon on board a convoy of tank-transporters. The huge convoy would make a three-day voyage (in the course of which a number of telephone and power lines had to be dismantled and put up again) to the nursery in Versailles, where the trees were to remain until being finally replanted at La Villette.

## MAY 1984

### The definitive design

On 16 April, I.M. Pei submitted a new draft of the "definitive" design. This featured a seven-meter sided square layout grid, but time was running short; the surveyors' plans for the interiors of the buildings had been drawn up, except for the detailed plans of the Richelieu wing which still housed the Finance Ministry. On 2 May 1984, the designer submitted an initial series of diagrams showing

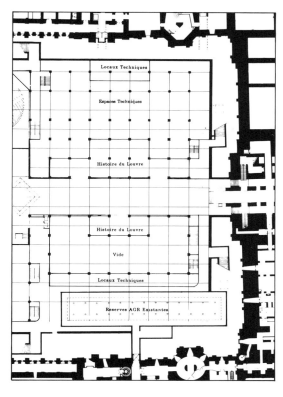

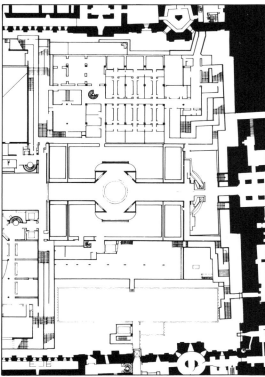

*Cour Napoleon*
*Plan of the mezzanine*
*before and after*
*discovery of*
*the Le Vau wall:*
*although the wall*
*fortunately did not encroach*
*upon the temporary*
*exhibition rooms*
*located beneath*
*the reception level,*
*a third of the project*
*still had*
*to be redesigned.*

the location of the main service networks; this was the signal for the technical design office to set to work!

Although the detailed design scheme would not be completed until early July, I.M. Pei's draft enabled work on the contract to proceed notwithstanding: it was possible to select the parties with whom the contract could be negotiated. This would need to be revised, notably with regard to the initial cost estimate for the works. Consultation accordingly took place between 4 May and 23 May 1984.

### Comprehensive siteworks insurance

It was now time to insure the various participants in the project. The *établissement public du Grand Louvre* and its collaborators – the architects, technical design offices, supervisory bodies, contractors, sub-contractors and suppliers involved in the project – might all be liable for eventual damages. Although the state was its own insurer, the risks involved by the works on the palace, the costs incurred by any eventual damages, and the definition of liabilities in a project on such a scale, were all factors which led the client body – as in other major projects – to subscribe to a comprehensive siteworks insurance policy in addition to the mandatory insurance taken out by each of the participants. In this way, should any problem arise, the settlement of insurance claims would not require any prior definition of liability.

The Lange insurance office – specialists in such operations – were called in to examine the various options and advise upon procedure. The aim was to provide insurance coverage before civil engineering works began in the cour Carrée in early 1985. A relevant clause – setting out the agreed insurance procedure – was straight away included in the draft engineering contract.

The competitors had three weeks in which to submit *"a technical memorandum and a theoretical breakdown which would allow assessment of their clear understanding of the specific problems involved in the project"*, cost estimates for the works, the amount of their fees, along with *"the time limits and the methods proposed for the conduct of the design work"*. Following scrutiny, two teams were short-listed ; finally, the Serete-Sogelerg team was chosen on 20 June 1984.

## JULY 1984

### Negociations

Three weeks were left to negotiate the contract. Engineering contracts included a provision called a complexity coefficient: this coefficient linked the designers' fees to the complexity of the works – the more complex the works involved, the higher the coefficient.

The average coefficient for the other major projects was eight; negotiations, therefore, started

out on this basis. Although separate cost estimates had been carried out for architects and technical design offices, and the respective contracts had been clearly defined, there remained some gaps and grey areas to be straightened out.

Moreover, the estimates would have to be adjusted to take account of the architects' proposed fees and the detailed scheme which, although still in the design process, was now quantifiable. First of all, a balance was drawn up between the figures proposed by the architects and the technical design offices; this was then compared with the estimates provided by the three separate cost analyses which had been carried out (by the technical design office which was part of the project team, by the Semah and by the client body); as a result, a cost ceiling of 1 120 000 000 FF was decided upon, along with an initial estimate of 1 003 003 755 FF – in other words, 6% higher than the first estimate submitted by the architects and technical design offices.

Henceforth – the initial estimate having been calculated – the total amount of fees was an arithmetic factor of the complexity coefficient. Like the estimates for the works, these fees had been calculated separately by the architects and technical design offices. Once the apportioning of the various tasks and the corresponding fees had been balanced out, the complexity coefficient of the total fees submitted was much higher than eight.

The reason for this was that the American team involved had never before worked in France and was unfamiliar with French methods. The working drawings for the National Gallery had been all-inclusive – right down to the very nuts and bolts used. In other words, the National Gallery project covered *all* of the detailed technical specifications and construction drawings, whereas only *some* of

*New York,*
*600 Madison Avenue,*
*8 July 1984, 3 p.m.:*
*"Where do I sign ?"*
*The flight back to Paris*
*leaves in two hours time.*

*Left hand page*
*Hoarding around*
*the cour Napoléon.*
*The Ecole des beaux-arts*
*is only a brush-stroke*
*away across the Seine.*

*Cour Napoléon*
*Two years after the theory*
*comes the practice:*
*grading the level* (top)
*and pumping*
*the water table* (bottom)
*on site (see p. 55).*

these were included at the Grand Louvre. Negotiations were complicated by another fundamental snag: I.M. Pei's office was in New York, whereas the other partners were based in Paris. I.M.Pei was in charge of the design work, but he couldn't permanently absent himself from his New York offices at 600 Madison Avenue, with their staff of two hundred architects.

Therefore, the first preliminary scheme for the cour Napoléon, and the first detailed scheme for the pyramid and surrounding fountains were drawn up in New York. Other design work was carried out in Paris where I.M.Pei set up a local office. Additional costs – to cover transatlantic return flights, Parisian accommodation and living expenses – all had to be written into the engineering contract. Moreover, the breakdown of design deadlines, a list of drawings to be submitted as the design process evolved, and a dozen other points all remained to be settled.

### Time's winged chariot hurrying near

On the afternoon of Friday 6 July 1984, the client body representative and three of the other four members of the steering team flew to New York. They had to clinch the contract within forty eight hours – in time for it to be submitted to the *commission spécialisée des Marchés de l'État* (Select Committee on State Contracts) which was due to meet on 27 July 1984. The deadline for submission was noon the following Monday, otherwise everything would have to be postponed until September 1984.

The meeting began as soon as they arrived at 600 Madison Avenue. They had until 3 p.m. on Sunday – it would take an hour to sign the contract, and another hour to get back to Kennedy Airport. In the course of discussions, it was agreed that 50% of the detailed technical specifications and of the construction drawings would be included in the contract; the American team agreed to reduce its fees accordingly. Differences emerged concerning the question of costs involved in the setting up of a local Parisian office. Finally, it was decided that no fixed provision would be made ; instead, the costs would be re-imbursed later as expenses, with the provision that such expenses should not exceed the initial estimate.

The contract was systematically gone through, point by point, in the course of discussions which – allowing for the occasional break – went on until 10 p.m. on the Friday, and then were resumed all day Saturday. By Saturday evening, the only unresolved question concerned the apportioning of 0,1% of the total fees. The total sum had been agreed upon with the client, but it remained to be decided whether the architects or the technical design office should accept a reduction in fees; on grounds of principle, neither party accepted to back down. And fatigue was taking its toll. After a further two hours, a 50-50 reduction was decided upon.

At 8 a.m. on Sunday, the contract was typed out again, and once more gone through page by page, with the help of excellent coffee provided by the secretary. By 3 p.m. the final page was typed out and the joint signing procedure began. It would take a whole hour for the four out of the five future co-partners to sign and initial the one-hundred and five-page contract.

Given the time difference, the flight back would arrive at Charles de Gaulle Airport at 8 a.m. local Paris time. It would still be 2 a.m. in New York. In four hours, the contract would be rushed from the airport to Paris, to be signed by the fifth partner; twenty copies would be made and the documents – along with the detailed program (which had been completed at 8 a.m. that morning) – would be delivered to boulevard Saint Germain by ten past noon. The duty officer – who had been asked to wait on especially by the programmer, J. Dourdin – had gone off for lunch, but formally took delivery of the file at 2 p.m.

That Monday 9 July 1984, the first operational phase of the project – involving a program, an inventory of givens, and a contract – was completed within the six-month deadline.

Or almost. Because another contract, also signed by the client body, would be required before the next phase – the design work proper – could begin. This would not be possible until the administrative procedure had followed its course. The Select Committee on State Contracts would first have to scrutinize the documents, any observations the Committee made would need to be taken into consideration, and there would have to be a firm commitment to the financial ceiling stipulated in the contract. It was only because the designers agreed to set to work before such administrative procedures were completed, that the design process could actually begin.

*Cour Napoléon*
*The four architectonic*
*concrete support posts*
*for the pyramid.*
*Two are in the process*
*of being poured,*
*while the two others*
*(to the right)*
*are ready and encased*
*in protective wooden shells.*
*Rear left:*
*the existing*
*Greco-Roman Antiquities*
*reserves can be seen beneath*
*the site offices.*

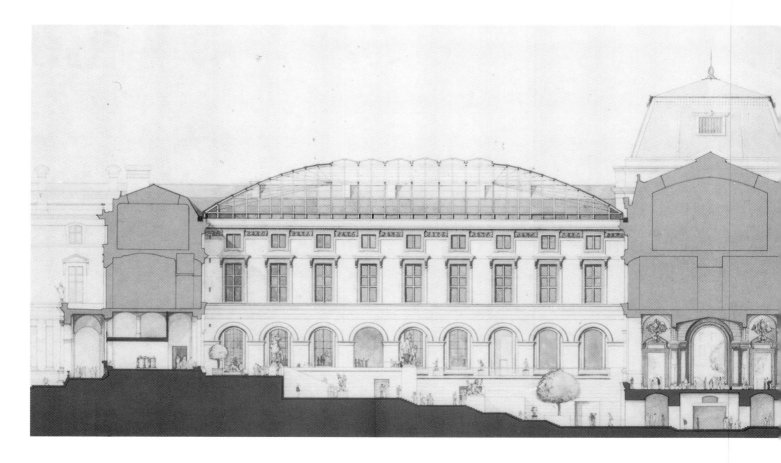

### Organization

2 p.m., Monday 9 July 1984: the pace was quickening. Now, instead of only fifteen, there were a hundred and fifty people working on the project. In the short term, the respective preliminary schemes for the cour Carrée, the cour Napoléon, and the Richelieu wing were due to be submitted by mid-September, mid-October, and mid-November 1984.

Before then, a number of posts still had to be filled in the flow chart defining the chain of command. To begin with, there were the posts of technical controller and site supervisor for the cour Carrée, since it would not be possible – given the time limit – to allocate sole overall supervision for the cour Carrée, the Cour Napoléon, and the Richelieu wing. Then, more posts would have to be attributed among the client body team; in this case, outside personnel would need to be hired, since the number of posts normally available for such appointments was not sufficient.

In any event, as planning was to proceed space by space (cour Carrée, cour Napoléon, and Richelieu wing), and as the corresponding design schemes were to be submitted at different dates, the client body team would set up a combined organization for all the spaces to be treated: the head of the design section would co-ordinate a team, each member of which would be responsible for one specific aspect of the whole project – the compatibility between program and proposed scheme, security provisions, civil engineering works, technical facilities, finishing works, time limits and costs, roadworks and various service networks, logistics etc. The entire team would attend co-ordination meetings with the designer; the studiously arranged distribution of architects and engineers seated in the conference room meant that each member could be kept fully informed of progress and could maintain a continuous overview of the whole project.

This was vital, since, at that point, the design process involved five separate teams working on their own section of the project in five different places – in New York, three areas of Paris, and in Lisieux. The design co-ordinator would have his work fully cut out; overlapping responsibilities would have to be clearly demarcated and apportioned. For the purpose of the works, the client body set up two departments, responsible respectively for the exterior and interior of the palace – two quite different areas. These teams would be expanded on completion of the design stage, once tenders were put out for the design of technical facilities and finishing works. In this way, continuity would be ensured. Once introductions had been made, the information necessary for design work to proceed had been handed on, a schedule drawn up for the provision of whatever technical information and designs were still required, and their own replacements organized, the two principal negotiating teams in the contract proceedings took a break.

### The heart of the matter

At the first co-ordination meeting which took place four weeks later, the whole atmosphere was quite different. The team had reached the heart of the matter and could take stock of the complexity involved. Everyone agreed to remain polite, to "verbally iron out" any eventual recriminations, and to set to work. Already, there was no shortage of subjects on the agenda. The air-conditioning and ventilation of the Napoléon reception area, for example, would require extractor flues with a 30 m$^2$ overall cross section – the equivalent of a Metro tunnel built vertically.

. . . . . . . . . . . . . . . . . . . . . . . . . . . . . . . . . . . . . . . . . . .

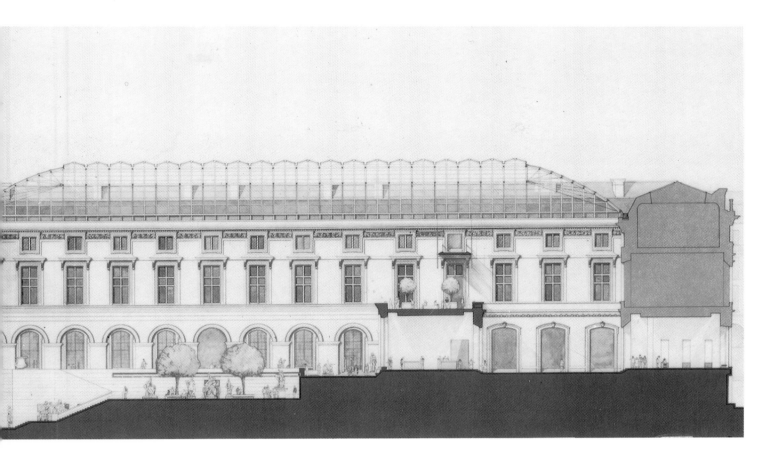

## MARCH 1985

### The *berlinoise*, Monsieur Le Vau and the detailed preliminary scheme

On the morning of 18 March 1985, traffic was diverted from the place du Carrousel and work on the *berlinoise* began. The *berlinoise* was a retaining wall to be built from the top down; construction involved boring holes at regular intervals and inserting steel structural sections, the lower ends of which were then sealed. Two meters of earth would then be removed, wire netting would be laid between the sections, and concrete poured. A further two metres of earth would then be removed, and so on. The structural sections were progressively anchored using tie-rods. Service networks, fire access, the phasing of works – these were just some of the reasons for parking the platform truck carrying the auger at the end of the cour Napoléon. Drilling began at the foot of the Sully pavilion, but did not get far. Before one meter below ground level was reached, the auger struck more than two meters of masonrywork.

Drilling stopped, and the earth was cleared away to reveal the top of a wall over one and a half meters wide.

Although they had no idea how far the wall extended, the archaeologists immediately realized what had been struck. The wall corresponded to what was previously thought to have been an uncompleted project by Le Vau. This project, however, *had* quite obviously been built. Such being the case, it would be the same height as the Philippe Auguste moat – about seven meters – and there was no reason to suppose that it would not continue running south, towards the Seine; it was an outwork following the line of the west counterscarp of Philippe Auguste's fortified castle.

Submission of the detailed preliminary scheme was scheduled for 8 May 1985 – a mere six weeks away.

There had already been delays with the safety design work; the architects' drawings ought to have been definitive since mid-February; now the longest of the three main access-ways from the reception area was closed off.

Again, once the scheduled opening of the cour Carrée took place at the end of the year, the sole access to the underpinning works below would be from this side, at the foot of the Sully pavilion. As for the emergency exits, the designer had just found a way of providing these without detracting from either the interior or exterior architecture – a one meter gradient for disabled visitors and for fire-engines was to be provided at ground level. Finally, the newly discovered wall would obstruct the clearance guage of the *voie de desserte intérieure*, Vdi, (internal service route). The problem was not only tri-dimensional, it affected cost and time feasibility.

By comparison, the problem raised by the nearby salle Saint Louis – under the salle des Caryatides – which formed part of the future underground circuit and which could not be laid out without work being carried on its ceiling (thus requiring the Vénus de Milo to be moved) – appeared a mere trifle. There were weeks like that.

In early April 1985, with all the inventories drawn up, it was decided that the technical design offices would go ahead, using the architects' drawings of 8 March which featured neither the Le Vau wall, nor the central security unit to be provided in the Richelieu wing, nor the amendments which had been suggested by certain users. By 1 July 1985, the drawings were to be amended so as to incorporate all these new features.

*Richelieu wing, June 1986*
*The project is ready,*
*the contractors await only*
*their contracts*
*to begin work;*
*the decision is taken,*
*however, to postpone works:*
*the Ministry of Finance*
*is not moving out*
*of the building (see p. 79).*

69

## MAY 1985

### The full-scale mockup

Before the application for a building permit – which had been submitted in late January 1985 – could be finally approved, two recommendations were necessary. The *Préfecture de police* had already notified its consent; for its part, the City of Paris – via the Mayor – had just requested that a full-scale mockup of the pyramid be made before the City could grant building permission.

Nothing could have been simpler: the archaeological dig was in full progress on the site of the future pyramid; half of the eventual base was covered with walls and three-meter-deep excavations, and work was due to begin on the other half. The request only called for a mockup, but how was one to put in place an object – some twenty meters high and thirty meters wide at its base – incorporating components which would be sufficiently thick to be plausible in the eyes of the public, and at the same time avoid displaying the object in a way that would confuse judgement? The solution was to use the largest crane in Europe (so as not to spoil the demonstration) to hoist a meshwork of nylon cables (for lightness) clad with heating pipe insulation components (for thickness) on a temporary deck (to avoid the excavations).

From 1 May to 5 May 1985, thousands of Parisians were thus able to see for themselves that the actual effect of the pyramid indeed corresponded to that which featured in the perspective drawings by I.M.Pei.

The cables were solidly anchored to concrete bollards on the ground; the pyramid had therefore to be hoisted just high enough that it did not appear to slump, yet not so high that it would overturn the crane. For similar reasons, there ought not be too much wind or rain.

For a week, the crane-driver could be seen perched in his cabin listening to the meteorological report, one eye on the anemometer, the other on the pyramid, his hands at the controls adjusting the pull on the cable each time the wind changed.

### The unique object

This was the period in which the design process reached its climax – when architecture, technical facilities, functioning and security all had to be combined to provide a unique object.

Until late each Tuesday afternoon, at the *établissement public*, the boardroom walls echoed to the discussions in the co-ordination meetings. Calmly but determinedly, the client body representatives, architects, and advisers responsible for programing, technical control and site supervision, along with a few others – some twenty to thirty people – would argue their respective cases.

In the photo of the site taken a fortnight later, on 28 May 1985 – despite the discovery of the Le Vau wall, submission date for the detailed preliminary scheme – all that could be seen was

*Cour Napoléon
The honeycomb
architectonic concrete
ceiling being cleaned
using acidified water.
In order to compensate
for deflection,
the truss rods on either end
of the main supporting
beams apply a force
equivalent to the weight
of the still
uncompleted pyramid.*

a cloud of dust. The client body nonetheless submitted to the designer twenty eight pages of general observations along with one hundred and forty two pages of remarks of a detailed nature.

Although at this point, given the tight schedule, it was impossible to fully integrate the Le Vau wall, design work continued at an uninterrupted pace.

Above all, however, the clarity and sensitivity of the extremely straightforward architectural approach adopted by I.M. Pei belied the intense work and the extraordinary complexity involved in the process. Nothing is more difficult to engineer than the patently obvious.

For the five million visitors, the reception area was to be the antechamber to the palace: priority was therefore given to public spaces. Thus, the first ''definitive'' design drawn up ten months previously had featured a symmetrical treatment to the entrance under the pyramid; twin escalators, arranged on either side of the belvedere, linked the ground level to the reception area, while at the top, a staircase wound round the elevator. Down below, however, a quarter of the reception area was cluttered with posts.

At the detailed preliminary design stage, the two escalators had been located together on one side, whereas the spiral staircase and the elevator had been provided symmetrically opposite. Shortly later, once the tip of the belvedere was firmly supported by a large post, civil engineering design work allowed for unified treatment of the entire hall space.

Similarly, I.M.Pei's self-imposed constraint – concerning the visitors' view of the palace from the reception level – meant that the spaces to be provided lacked sufficient headroom.

He therefore modified the volumes at the start of design work on the detailed preliminary scheme: the auditorium would occupy the entire volume of the reception and mezzanine levels; the Louvre shop – originally planned on two levels – would assume a cubic shape; the temporary exhibitions spaces would be superimposed exactly over the History of the Louvre section; the floor of the temporary exhibitions spaces would be lowered to the bottom level of the plenum so as to gain an extra meter in height; the respective accesses to the spaces would communicate visually by the provi-

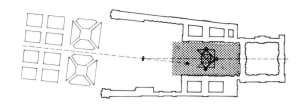

Left
*The honeycomb ceiling.*
*Oregon pine shuttering*
*– prime choice*
*for its regular grain –*
*sealed, sandpapered,*
*polished and protected*
*by a plastic sheet*
*during the assembly*
*of the reinforcement grid;*
*the iron bars*
*were suspended*
*so as to leave no trace;*
*technical components*
*were integrated.*
*Architectonic concrete*
*was poured*
*non-stop day and night*
*between joints*
*to prevent*
*construction joints*
*from forming.*

Right
*View down*
*to one of the corners*
*of the pyramid scaffolding;*
*behind, the intersecting*
*support beams*
*and the honeycomb*
*shuttering.*

sion of a circular hollow feature – the spaces would meet at the four extremities to provide the volume required for the display of large exhibits. In that way, the longest of the three main routes from the reception area ceased to resemble a corridor.

I.M. Pei's approach unfailingly prevailed, and the result – as in the case of the Washington National Gallery – is manifest. Concerning the Grand Louvre, however, the essential difference lay in the time-limit involved. Ten years of design work had gone into the 56 000 m² Washington project; here, only five years were available to design a 70 000 m² project.

### The complexity of the straightforward approach

The public space to be given priority treatment featured a floor, walls and a ceiling.

The nine-meter deep walls were to be treated in stonework like the foundations of the surrounding palace; the faultlessly arranged stonework would provide the unique, stark decorative feature throughout.

The floor would receive a similarly rigorous treatment. Although few of the visitors would see it, they would all feel it: the square pattern of the floor would provide an exact counterpoint to the diamond-shaped panes of the pyramid, just as – although a different scale – the fountain basins

echoed the shape of the reception hall below and the sloping sides of the pyramid above.

The ceiling could only be treated in concrete, in order to achieve a flat surface. As was the case with the posts supporting the pyramid and the lintels of the wall openings, the concrete would be exposed, and therefore architectonic – in other words, carefully graded, tinted and applied.

In order to enhance the perception of space and light, this huge blank page would have to be embellished. The air-conditioning, smoke-extraction, fire-detection, and lighting systems would call for a vast amount of appliances, ducts and wiring to be integrated. The location of the outlets required by such features would be barely perceptible to visitors. The ceiling of the reception area would be treated in a rigorous honeycomb design, corresponding to the three routes – to the collections, the shopping arcade leading to the car-park, and to the auditorium; in short throughout the entire volume of the twin height spaces.

This was a nightmare for the technical design offices: the spans involved were more on the scale of a civil engineering project than that of a mere building project; the location of technical components such as air-conditioning vents and fire-detection units was strictly unalterable; the ceiling and floor thicknesses had been cut down to the strict minimum (a 1/27 factor of the total span) so

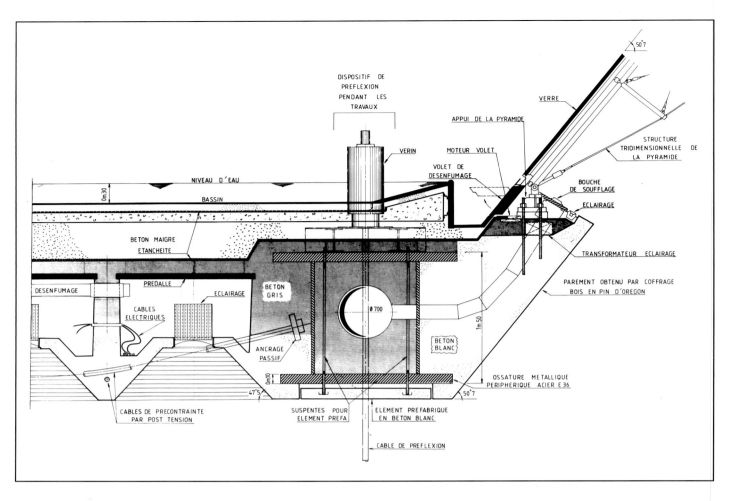

DISPOSITIF DE PREFLEXION PENDANT LES TRAVAUX

VERIN

NIVEAU D'EAU

0m30

BASSIN

BETON MAIGRE ETANCHEITE

DESENFUMAGE

PREDALLE

ECLAIRAGE

CABLES ELECTRIQUES

BETON GRIS

ANCRAGE PASSIF

47°5

CABLES DE PRECONTRAINTE PAR POST TENSION

SUSPENTES POUR ELEMENT PREFA

ELEMENT PREFABRIQUE EN BETON BLANC

CABLE DE PREFLEXION

APPUI DE LA PYRAMIDE

MOTEUR VOLET

VOLET DE DESENFUMAGE

VERRE

STRUCTURE TRIDIMENSIONNELLE DE LA PYRAMIDE

BOUCHE DE SOUFFLAGE

ECLAIRAGE

TRANSFORMATEUR ECLAIRAGE

PAREMENT OBTENU PAR COFFRAGE BOIS EN PIN D'OREGON

Ø 700

1m50

BETON BLANC

0m10

OSSATURE METALLIQUE PERIPHERIQUE ACIER E 36

50°7

50°7

*The complexity of the straightforward approach. Section showing the foot of the pyramid, supporting beam, water basins and honeycomb ceiling. The omega-shaped springs designed to muffle the sound of the water jets – notably in the auditorium – are not featured.*

that there was no room for the air-conditioning ducts which were re-located in the walls; expansion joints were to be integrated into the overall pattern; fresh air intakes and used air vents had to cross the plenum system which was turned into a technical deck running two meters below the ceiling. The latter feature, at least, ought to overcome the initial objection concerning the installation and maintenance of service networks, but the geohydrological computer simulation would have to be run through again to ensure that the water table threshold had not been crossed; furthermore, in the event of two ducts crossing each other, the two meter gap would have to be altered again. Finally, this was a space accessible to the general public and thus subject to complex safety regulations: accesses, intersections, emergency exits, etc. The number of new design problems to be tackled was endless.

### The entrance on the Tuileries garden side

It was decided that there would be no building around the arc de triomphe in the place du Carrousel, in the area where the chestnut trees grew. These trees had been planted in the nineteenth century and were an essential feature visible to anyone strolling towards the cour Napoléon from the Tuileries gardens.

The Tuileries gardens had been laid out to the west, on the axis of the former Tuileries palace; to the east, this axis ran past the site of the former palace and ended in the middle of the Lescot wing which, however, was not laid out parallel to the old Tuileries. When Henri IV planned to extend the cour Carrée, the axis had been shifted, and this had

been concealed by developments between the Louvre and Tuileries palaces.

A few centuries later, in 1871, when the Tuileries palace was gutted and demolished, the axis could be clearly seen to be out of line with the perspective from the Champs-Elysées. Trees were therefore planted around the small arc de triomphe and in the two squares in order to mask what was, at that time, regarded as a visual defect.

Objections might have been raised to the pyramid had its volume been visible from this major axis, thus spoiling the view of the palace. The chestnut trees and the arc de triomphe, however, formed a kind of narrow diaphragm, which I.M.Pei – as early as his preliminary sketch – had sealed off with a statue placed to the fore of the cour Napoléon.

The pyramid itself was wedged right in the centre of the cour Napoléon and its tip was lower than the palace eaves. Thus, it was not until one passed the arc de triomphe du Carrousel that it came into view, resembling a sculpture standing in the middle of its square.

As soon as the archaeological excavations were over (the archaeologists would have loved to have stayed on for another twenty years), earthworks had immediately began and, for a while, the bottom of the cour Napoléon was filled with a superb lake of green water. 21 June 1985 was the day the annual "festival of music" was celebrated; that evening, amidst the noise of the buses passing on the other side of the hoardings, the archaeologists held a party and a barbecue on the site. It was an enchanted, slightly surrealistic scene – on the edge of a lake, in the remnants of the excavation site, surrounded by the façades of the Louvre, a hundred archaeologists danced to the sounds of the latest hits.

. . . . . . . . . . . . . . . . . . . . . . . . . . . . . . . . . . . . . . . . . . . . . . . . .

## OCTOBER 1985

### The definitive estimate

On Monday 7 October 1985, the final details of the definitive cost estimate were submitted to the client body. At that stage of design and works, this involved a final cost estimate for the cour Carrée, together with an estimate for the detailed preliminary scheme for the Denon wing. This estimate of the final cost differed, naturally, from that submitted by the designer and site supervisor for the cour Carrée. After a cost savings analysis had been conducted, the estimate for the Denon wing came to twice more than had been provided for. In any event, the total estimate exceeded the 95% of the cost ceiling stipulated in the contract.

Both the designer and the client body acknowledged a share of responsibility for having gone over the cost ceiling, and therefore negociations began. The task involved identifying and calculating possible cost-saving measures, as well as identifying any costly modifications which had not been foreseen in the initial program. The financial ceiling was a firm figure which had been thoroughly checked – including in the course of design work.

On the other hand, the financial envelope – which had been fixed at two thousand million francs in the engineering contract – meant that the limit of 95% of the ceiling price could not be altered, and would have to include any modifications to the program. In the first tentative, round of discussions, only the technical design offices submitted a detailed breakdown of possible cost-saving measures, and these would only allow for a mere ten million francs to be economized.

The procedure necessary to get siteworks launched had meant that numerous orders had been placed, mainly in the case of the cour Carrée where the works had encountered many obstacles – notably due to the service networks. The client body team drew up a list of these orders, and then spent a whole day sorting out into two categories: on the one hand, those already provided for within the largest cost; on the other for which no such provision had been made.

The final cost estimate for the cour Carrée was gone over with a fine-tooth comb. However, there was little hope of economizing on works which were virtually completed in the cour itself, and which might well incur further costs when the underpinning works under the palace were carried out. Moreover, in three months time, the sole access to the site would be via the cour Napoléon; it was impossible to determine a schedule which would satisfy the constraints encountered by both parties.

*The complexity of the straightforward approach (contd.) Preparing to pour the concrete casing for the supporting beams. The integrated blow duct in the beam supplies air pipes that are designed notably to prevent condensation on the pyramid glazing.*

There still remained the cour Napoléon and the Richelieu wing. The architects' fees had been particulary generous, due partly to the way in which the architects had been commissioned, and partly to the time limit involved in the calculation of their initial costs. The advisers to the client body reckoned that the amount that the architects had overcharged was roughly equal to the shortfall for the technical contracts. As a result of a four-hour-meeting – in the course of which it was consistently requested that cost savings be carried out – a few million francs were economized. The situation had reached a deadlock.

That was the situation on 11 October 1985, when the client body gave its approval to the detailed preliminary scheme for the cour Napoléon. Indeed, the atmosphere had cooled off distinctly since May. In actual fact, two whole months of design work would be required in addition to the schedule submitted in late August 1985. In essence, this extra work involved tackling a few remaining reservations which had been raised by the Safety Committee, obtaining official approval for the platform under the pyramid, and finding a sufficiently large space for the main ticket-office.

At half past twelve on Thursday 17 October 1985, the negociators locked themselves away in one of the offices of the *établissement public du Grand Louvre*. The chief representative for the client body

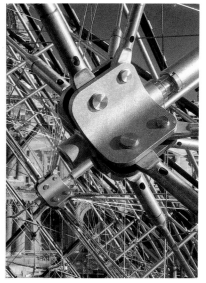

*The structure
of the pyramid.
Depending
on the vantage point,
the structure looks
extremely simple
or highly complicated.*

scrutinized. After eighteen months of feverish activity, all present were fully acquainted with the project.

Telephone calls were made to specialists whenever important points had to be elucidated, or detailed figures were required. By mid-afternoon, the estimates had been examined three times in succession, brought into line and set in order: furnishings and duplicated accounts were eliminated, the amounts charged for fees had been adjusted or clarified, and the estimate was calculated at 1 166 million francs.

The fundamental issue – how to reduce costs by cutting down on expensive elements – was then broached. This issue had been looming for several weeks, and the question gradually emerged in the course of a lengthy fourth round of discussions. The estimate was reduced to 1 115 million francs. Later that night, a further round of negociations brought the estimated cost down to 1 089.6 million francs, and the range of possible cost-saving measures was exhausted.

The only remaining possibility available to the client body was to postpone certain aspects of the program in order to partially offset certain costly modifications – the Le Vau wall, for example – which had cropped up in the course of design work. This was mooted in the sixth stage of talks and, finally, it was decided to sacrifice the protection facilities in the workshops for which the Museum Technical Director had applied at the stage of the detailed preliminary scheme. Fixed at 1 063.678 million francs, the definitive estimate was within 1 064 million francs threshold corresponding to the 95% of the financial ceiling.

It was 4.30 a.m. The minutes of the meeting were photocopied and handed out.

Tenders for the civil engineering works and the air-conditioning in the cour Napoléon were to be launched a few hours later.

### The flood of contracts out to tender

It was no time to relax. In the course of the following weeks each new bid would have to be individually examined, and all outstanding points cleared up. While specific problems were being sifted through one by one, others of a more comprehensive nature – such as security measures, the technical deck, or the main ticket-office – would need to be solved. The decisions adopted during the all-night session of 17 October would have to be implemented. Moreover, the designer's estimate for each contract would have to be compared to the detailed estimate; fees would need to be checked; the shortfalls for each contract would have to be identified, and covered. Finally, there could be no let up in supervising the co-ordination of works affecting the transition from one area to another of the project.

prepared to take note of each agreed point as the meeting progressed.

Negociations started out on the basis of the estimate submitted by the designer; this was examined along with the detailed preliminary schemes for the cour Napoléon and the Richilieu wing, the preliminary scheme for the Denon wing, and the contracts for the cour Carrée. Together with the official minutes of the meeting, these elements would constitute the final document. Each term was carefully considered. As each point was noted down, it was read out aloud for approval or rejection.

Each contract in each area was taken up and

*A sailing ship's rigging?
Yes, but with perfectly
accurate assembly
tolerances: wind
or no wind,
these sails have
to remain flat.*

## DECEMBER 1985

### The design stage draws to an end

On 10 December 1985, the fiftieth co-ordination meeting took place between the client body, and the architectural and design team set up by the contract – I.M. Pei, Duval, Macary, Serete and Sogelerg.

After countless difficulties, the cour Carrée was on the point of completion. The major fabric and roof works, and the restoration of the façades, were finished. The twenty two leading master-masons in France, along with a hundred highly skilled workmen, had left the site; the weatherproof awnings and the scaffolding had been dismantled. For the past month, work had been proceeding rapidly in the courtyard where granite slabs and traditional paving stones were being laid. An increasing number of archaeological finds had been made on site. Trial bores had been sunk at the foot of the pavillon des Arts in an attempt to locate Philippe Auguste's defensive wall, but these had proved fruitless. It was impossible to clear the moat away at that point: access had to be kept open to the façades and to the roofs, but the well had collapsed a few centimeters away from the wall which was still intact. As a result, the passage between the castle moat and the anteroom leading to the elevators had had to be modified.

The vibrations struck unexpectedly. While works were in progress on the *voie de desserte intérieure* (internal service route), a few meters away – and despite the supporting stay bars – a ten-meter section of the counterscarp face in the square moat collapsed in the presence of members of the *commission des Monuments historiques* who were on an official visit that very day.

Eleven contracts concerning the cour Napoléon had been combed through and were out to tender; within a fortnight, another eight were expected to be ready for the launching of works on the Richelieu wing. The technical design office for the laboratory facilities and the delivery area had been selected, and design work could begin. Work had begun on the conversion of the avenue Lemonnier into an underpass, a financially viable framework had been adopted within which design work on the Denon wing could proceed, and negotiations were underway on the question of the link-up to the cold-air facility in Les Halles. The only remaining unresolved issue concerned the self-contained emergency power generator. The centre of gravity of the project was moving away from the design stage toward the works stage.

By the evening of 31 December 1985 – apart from a few odd square meters of granite slabs – the cour Carrée was completed.

The project for civil engineering works in the cour Napoléon was submitted on 24 January 1986. The Central State Commission on public contracts informed the *établissement public* of its approval. Three weeks later, works were out to tender.

On 17 February, the contract was awarded to the Dumez company, only seventeen days after the date which had been decided upon two years earlier; henceforth it would no longer be fifteen people, as in January 1984, nor one hundred and fifty people, as in the summer of that year, but now one thousand five hundred people who would develop the project.

. . . . . . . . . . . . . . . . . . . . . . . . . . . . . . . . . . . . . . . . . . . . . . . . . . . . . . .

## JUNE 1986

### The seventh phase of the Richelieu wing

On 24 June 1986, uncertainty still reigned as to whether or not contracts for the Richelieu wing could be signed, when suddenly the decision was made known: the reception scheme was not called into question, but, in the Richelieu wing, the only works to be carried out were those which were vital to the opening of the cour Napoléon.

These included the link between the place du Palais-Royal and the reception area – at ground level, and via the lateral escalators. A swiftly conducted investigation showed also that, in order for the reception to function, the following works would be necessary: the four air extractor flues, the central security unit, the staff entrance by the articulation with the cour Carrée, a share of the

1. *March 1984*
*The archaeologists*
*arrive and the trees leave.*

2. *July 1985*
*Earthworks keep pace*
*with the archaeological*
*excavations.*

3. *December 1985*
*The final excavations.*

4. *October 1986*
*Arrival*
*of the first support beam*
*for the pyramid.*

5. *March 1987*
*All the beams are in place.*

6. *June 1987*
*The first arris*
*of the pyramid*
*is assembled on*
*a temporary scaffolding.*

7. *Early September 1987*
*The first glazed panels*
*are assembled.*

8. *Late September 1987*
*The shell is completed.*

9. *9 January 1988*
*Laying the ground level slabs*
*and paving stones.*

10. *July 1988*
*The basins just before*
*being filled with water.*

1

2

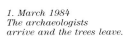

3

4

5

6

7

8

9

10

basement – the workshop program could not be carried out – temporary emergency exits in the Ministry, and highly complex re-routing of service networks.

All these works would be noisy and would have to be conducted at night, between 9 p.m. and 8 a.m. The twin extractor flues to be provided on either side of the Richelieu arcade would be temporary. The question was whether they ought to be located in the Ministry courtyards, or in the cour Napoléon. A relevant document would need to be drawn up in consultation with the Ministry in under three weeks; this document would have to be comprehensive and include a cost breakdown for design and works. The seventh phase of the Richelieu wing was about to get underway. There was no fanfare. There was no time for one !

Three weeks later, the temporary extractor flues – to be located in the cour du Ministre and in the cour des Caisses – were finally approved; retractable metal gates in the gallery giving onto the cour Napoléon would provide the two temporary emergency exits; and the central safety units would be omitted from the initially required areas in the Richelieu wing, so as to maintain access to the Ministry Staff Co-operative premises. The underpinning works necessary to provide the link between the reception area and the Richelieu arcade would be carried out within a sealed bell in order to cut down the noise: the Minister's office was on the floor above.

### Computer facilities

All this meant that the time required to launch design work on computer facilities was running out.

The position was straightforward: in both the short term and the medium term, it would be necessary to ensure an overall coherence between options, some of which had been chosen at an early stage of the project, others which were yet to be chosen. The questions of central technical management, security, the automatic switchboard, computer-assisted maintenance and ticket facilities were all already being dealt with, unlike the question of computerized backup at visitor receptions.

In the latter case, everyone agreed that it was important that – at the very least – information on which rooms were open and which were closed be available in the reception on opening day. In this way, visitors would not – as they still did – discover on arrival that the part of the museum they wished to visit was closed.

It was also obvious that there were major productivity gains to capitalize upon in the future cultural, administrative and financial running of the museum. Moreover, such computer facilities were already supposed to have been taken into account in the organizational studies instigated over a year earlier to provide an initial rough idea of the staff numbers which would be required by the various reception and museum functions.

Finally, there was a further peculiarity to the project: distances were great, and the various departments had still not been definitively – and in some case not even temporarily – located.

The position might well appear straightforward; the solution, on the other hand, was not obvious. It involved drawing up a master plan for the computer facilities to be provided in a place whose statute and organization were not yet defined; a place which was – and would be for the following ten years – undergoing a complete shakeup, and this in the absence both of the future decision-makers who would run the place, and of most of the museum users.

The only possible approach was to find out which computer facilities would be necessary to run the museum in a way which would provide maximum autonomy. This was a forward-looking approach since it was obvious that the future Louvre should be capable of managing its own affairs independently. Discussion soon became heated: there were many reasons for doing nothing. Despite all such obstacles, the tender for firms providing computer services was prepared; it was sufficiently wide-ranging in scope, as circumstances demanded.

## DECEMBER 1986

### An ordinary day

19 December 1986 was a day just like any other day. To be on the safe side, the designer had been asked to carry out a final check of the clearance in the internal service route. This confirmed that it would be impossible to move the display furniture into either the temporary exhibitions space or the history of the Louvre space: lintels, doors and service networks did not comply with the specified clearance dimensions – they were either too large, or inconveniently installed. 19 December 1986, therefore, was a day like any other day, had it not been for the fact that the decision had just been taken not to submit the tenders for visitors directions and computer facilities to the Select Committee on State Contracts for approval. In other words, that meant that that the reception would not be completed in February 1988: the civil engineering worksite was delayed by an extra three months – decisions concerning the statute and future running of the museum had not been taken; half of the budget required for furnishing and fitting out the reception was still to be approved; it was unlikely that the History of the Louvre space, the temporary exhibition spaces and the restaurants could be put into service before July 1988 at the earliest.

Three years of relentless work and the goal was not in sight. After six months of daily struggles and complications, something seemed to be snapping.

..................................................

## FEBRUARY 1987

### Second wind

In early 1987, following a month of gloom, there was a new lease of life.

The deadline had, after all, been made deliberately tight in order to ensure the definitive and irrevocable nature of an infinitely complex project. Only two thirds of the work scheduled in the first phase would be completed, but that in itself was an accomplishment, and the developing project possessed an intrinsic rationale which allowed it to progress.

Civil engineering works in the avenue du Général-Lemonnier, the laboratory facilities, and the delivery area, had begun since October and December 1968 respectively. Visitor directions, audio-visual facilities, and the automatic switch-board were in the process of design.

It only remained to launch the competition for the fitting out of the Louvre shop, and for the furnishing of the reception area. The other tenders had been awarded: the firm of Sema-Metra had been selected to design the computer facilities; Richard Peduzzi had received the contract for the interior layout of the space to be given over to the history of the Louvre; Jean-Michel Wilmotte had received a similar contract for the temporary exhibition spaces.

The master plan for the development of the Grand Louvre, drawn up in February 1987, not only included the opening of the reception area, it also demonstrated the overall coherence of the project. It set out the principal features of the project which had been completed or had yet to be completed. The plan covered programing, investment and functioning, and was fully backed up by figures and time schedules. Taking in restoration work on the palace, it proposed an estimate of three billion francs. In return for a level of investment constantly adjusted to future functioning costs (notably energy and security costs), the annual functioning budget would amount to some five hundred million francs, once the redeployment of the collections had been carried out.

Given an expected four to five million visitors, and provided that the museum was run independently and not as some government department,

*The pyramid in natural setting.*

then the revenue generated by a market-orientated commercial policy would cover more than half of expenditure.

Much had been done, and much remained to be done before such an ambition would be realized. It was more or less comparable to running the Alexandria Library as a profit-making concern.

### Descriptive Catalogues

Meanwhile, the preliminary inventory of the museum collections promised to take much longer than the survey of givens that had been carried out back in 1984. This time, more than six months would be required. Most of the work would have to be carried out inside the buildings, and the continued functioning of the museum would provide an additional constraint.

A start was made on setting up a descriptive computer file listing the contents of all the existing museum rooms and the eventual assignment of these contents in the new spaces. The obvious difficulty was to provide all-inclusive information giving the exact location, name, and new emplacement for each item.

Meanwhile, the Le Vau wall episode had one repercussion – work was begun on creating a file of historical plans of the Louvre which might eventually prove to be of technical interest. The plans in the files of the Head Palace Architect, the National Archives, and the Ministry of Finance were dug out and catalogued .The exact location (filing cabinet, drawer) of each item was carefully noted. Where necessary, duplicate copies were made as the inventory progressed. For four years, J.Dourdin had been involved in the overall programing of the Louvre, and had been assisting the client body in the examination of the design schemes; being thus ideally qualified to compile such data with a view to the future functioning and investment requirements of the museum, he was entrusted with the task. Besides, there were now four hundred hefty files, and six thousand drawings dealing with the project itself, and more data would be forthcoming. As it took each person new to the project several months to become fully operational, it was necessary to summarize and classify all this information. For the moment, however, there were too many other tasks to attend to.

*A spiral staircase
for those who do not want
to use the escalators.
A huge spring,
fixed at either end.*

## JUNE 1987

### The redeployment of the museum exhibits

While everyday business proceeded, consideration was given to the methods to be adopted in the palace, concerning the design and works to be carried out before the exhibits were redeployed. A nine-page memorandum was submitted on 11 June 1987, describing the general framework and the constraints, and proposing solutions to the specific problems which had been identified.

The general framework was straightforward. The Louvre was an historical monument, one wing of which – the Richelieu wing – had originally been built and laid out to accommodate the offices of the Imperial household. This wing was to be entirely redesigned and converted into a museum; work on the existing museum, on the other hand, involved the installation of technical facilities rather than any alteration to the interior layout. The entire works would take ten years and the museum would have to keep functioning; since the works would proceed within the building; redeployment would have to be undertaken in successive instalments – spaces would be first cleared, then re-arranged, then used again.

On the one hand, however, the Louvre actually consisted of five separate buildings (the cour Carrée, and the Denon, Richelieu, Flore and Marsan wings), linked together by narrow intersections which orchestrated the layout of the palace and governed the way it functioned; on the other hand, the existing – and future – boundaries between the collections did not correspond to such articulations. The Department of Oriental Antiquities, for example, was to be housed partly in the cour Carrée, and partly in the Richelieu wing.

During the redeployment process, at a number of levels, and in various domains – museology, technical facilities, interior architecture, visitor routes, security measures, investment and functioning costs, time limits etc. – it would be necessary to maintain overall consistency, despite the fact that redeployment would be carried out space by space. Moreover, serious discrepancies might arise owing to the size of the palace, the length of the operation, the sheer quantity and variety of techniques and information involved, the number of people concerned, the (mostly limited) tasks they would be executing, and the length, location and nature of such tasks, not to mention the technical and museological advances – and the necessary adaptation to these – which were almost bound to occur over a ten year period.

The respective requirements of the museum displays on the one hand, and those of the fitting out and functioning of the museum buildings on the other, would prove quite inconsistent in the course of a long process of re-arrangement, whereas the objective was to lay out a series of complemen-

tary departments and sub-departments. This incompatibility led to a distinction being drawn between primary technical investments (public accesses, goods-elevators, emergency exits, wet services and networks, technical premises etc.), and secondary technical investments (the layout of a series of rooms where all the works could be carried out within the volume of the room). The "secondary" areas would be linked to services provided in the adjacent "primary" areas.

As this distinction was not purely topological, it was necessary – in each building – to conduct investigations in order to identify and distinguish the two types of investment, as to their location, physical structure and financial implications. It would then be possible to draw up an ideal timetable for the primary investments – allowing notably for the sequence of departmental re-arrangement adopted – while specific works could proceed on the secondary investments without detracting from the overall coherence of the project. In order to achieve this, a data bank was to be created. This would be specifically tailored to handling the various schemes and the running of this museum; the skilled team of specialists in charge would gear the operation to the overall project. To ensure an optimum flow of information, the data bank (consisting of computerized data and print-outs) would be structured thematically and spatially. Information would be classified from the general to the particular, and dated so as not to loose sight of the final objective and the rationale governing successive choices.

### A fleeting pause for reflection

On 14 August 1987, Maurice Foissac, who had taken charge of works in the cour Napoléon, died in a senseless motorbike accident. He was 53, and his death was a bitter blow. In a place so soaked in history as the Louvre, it was impossible not to be conscious of human mortality, yet death always seemed somehow removed in time; brutally, it reminded us of its presence. For a long time – on site or in the office – we would suddenly recall Maurice's familiar features; we would pause for an instant and our pressing affairs would at once seem trivial, and then his smiling face would invite us to pursue our dream.

## DECEMBER 1987

### The History of the Louvre space

On 16 December 1987, in the studios of the théâtre des Amandiers in Nanterre, Richard Peduzzi presented a prototype of the layout of the History of the Louvre space, featuring floor, walls, ceiling and lighting. Amongst other difficulties, a series of joists – which had been included at one stage in the design process when the working drawings for the concrete structures had been drawn up – threatened to diminish the volume of the room and to complicate the artificial lighting of the proposed glazed roof. The full-scale prototype showed that this would not be the case.

The design stage, however, was not completed; nor was the cost factor finally settled. There had been some misunderstanding concerning the bas-reliefs by Jean Goujon which adorned the top of one of the façades in the *Ecole des beaux-arts*. These were intended to be an integral feature of the walls in the History of the Louvre space; unfortunately there were eight bas-reliefs, and not four, as had been originally believed. The relief maps showing the Louvre and the surrounding district at various periods posed problems of historical interpretation. Finally, complications had arisen in the negociations over capital losses incurred in the fixed-price contracts settled with I.M. Pei for the provision of the floor, walls and ceilings; and it was not clear how the revised fees should be calculated and included in the definitive costs.

### The temporary exhibition spaces

Similar problems arose in the case of the first temporary exhibition space, albeit not to the same degree. Ideally, the furnishings to be provided ought not only to be adaptable at the last minute for use in whatever exhibition was currently being mounted, they should also serve for the next exhibition scheduled to follow. The problem was basically financial. More exhibits were to be displayed than had been provided for in the contract. The provisional estimate for the proposed display exceeded the financial envelope which had been allocated. An initial difficulty concerned the type of wood proposed for the flooring and the pattern of the floors themselves; secondly, the doors had been altered to allow convenient access from the internal service route (Vdi).

The Louvre shop proved no exception: the floors and ceilings had been modified ; the original fitted carpeting had been replaced by stone, then by tiles, then by a combination of wood, stone and carpeting, etc.

The whole question of furnishings had gradually become obscured by concern with the layout. The final layout would be all the more successful, but it was unlikely that the inauguration deadline for these spaces – October 1988 – would be met.

### The Richelieu wing: phase 8

Work on the Richelieu wing - and along with it, the redeployment of all the collections located in the vicinity of the reception area – was running three

years late. A series of handicaps had repeatedly been encountered – including partially conducted and randomly abandoned design work, and a complicated time schedule requiring constant updating – and the resulting logjam had to be cleared. Preliminary design work had to go back to square one. As the whole process had already involved seven separate phases, the negociations over fees took some time – more than a year – but reached a successful conclusion. The amended contract merely required formal signing, and then the road ahead would be clear to resume overall design work on the Richelieu wing, despite the implications of the time schedule. The new arrangements at least introduced a more rational approach to the works proper, and meant that the design of the exhibition rooms would no longer be beset by technical hindrances. They were to be executed by I.M. Pei, in association with M. Macary and the Serete and Sogelerg technical design offices.

. . . . . . . . . . . . . . . . . . . . . . . . . . . . . . . . . . . . . . . . . . . . . . .

## APRIL 1988

### Detailed design work on the French painting collections

The detailed preliminary scheme for the east wing was submitted on 22 April 1988, and the architectural treatment was wholeheartedly approved.

The competition jury had already been impressed by the the overall layout propositions for the rooms; their judgement was confirmed.

In the southern part of the building, the treatment of the intersecting components of the wing highlighted the architectural history of the palace. The old south façade – which had bisected the wing longitudinally – now featured openings onto the Seine and the cour Carrée.

However, the second floor of the east wing had to be redesigned for structural reasons. The upper floor housed the wood panelling in the chambres du Roi and the *objets d'art* Department.

The access to the *objets d'art* Department had been considerably affected in the course of works on the north wing, and was once more called into question. This section of the department would either have to be entirely closed for nine months, or partially closed for two consecutive nine and seven month periods.

### Prior to the Presidential election

Meanwhile, bids had been submitted for the restaurant concessions. The proposed interior design required I.M. Pei's prior approval. Design work on visitor directions had proceeded full pace and was now completed. The contract was out to tender. In the place du Caroussel, works on the gallery required that traffic be temporarily re-routed on the cour Napoléon site. This temporary measure was to last three years.

As the Presidential election approached, the Finance Ministry completed the preliminary scheme for the rehousing of its offices in the east section of the Richelieu wing. The Ministerial Departments asked the *établissement public* authorities if it might be possible to obtain a 400 KW link-up to the cold air supply from the Halles facility. Ostensibly, they were not planning to leave the west wing in the near future. The color of the temporary extractor flue in the cour du Ministre had not been decided upon, and building permission had not been granted: little time remained before the scheduled testing of the air-conditioning system in the cour Napoléon. The executive of the Museum drew up a schedule – along similar lines to that drawn up by the *établissement public* – of the tasks it had to complete by the opening date of the reception area. In late June 1988, and in the light of these two separately established schedules, a precise date was settled for the opening. The new teams for the future museum were set up, ready to take over.

. . . . . . . . . . . . . . . . . . . . . . . . . . . . . . . . . . . . . . . . . . . . . . .

## JUNE 1988

### After the Presidential election

June 1988 – the Presidential election was over. The new master plan for the development of the Grand Louvre was on the drawing board. The Finance Ministry was to move out of its Louvre premises in a single operation scheduled for late 1989.

The Grand Louvre project would be completed within seven years.

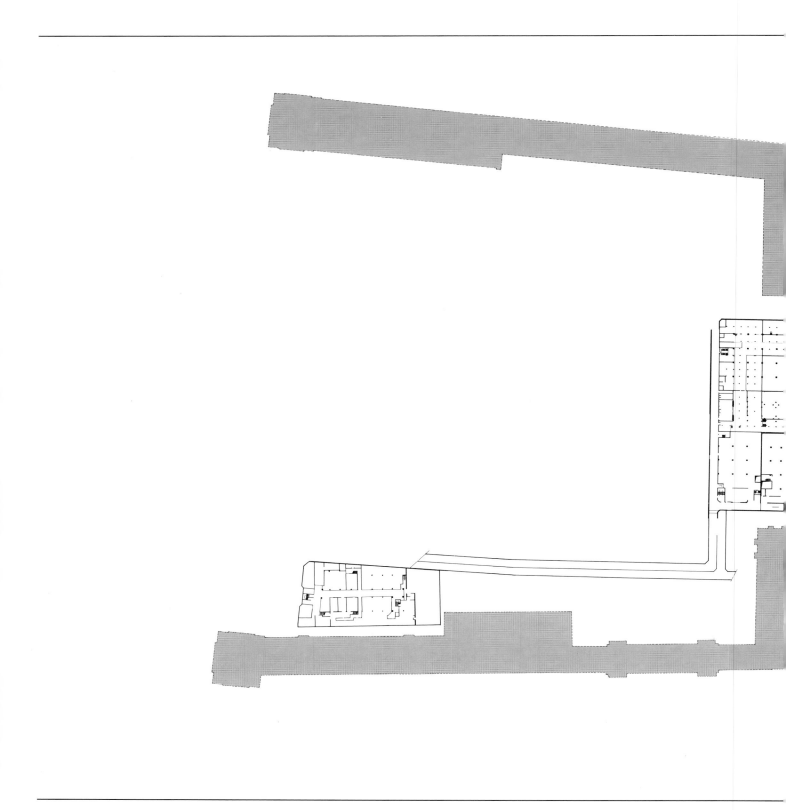

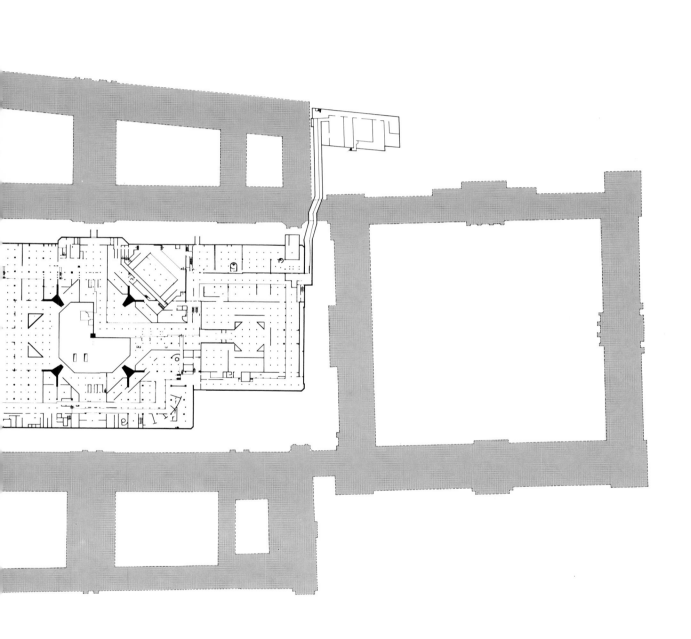

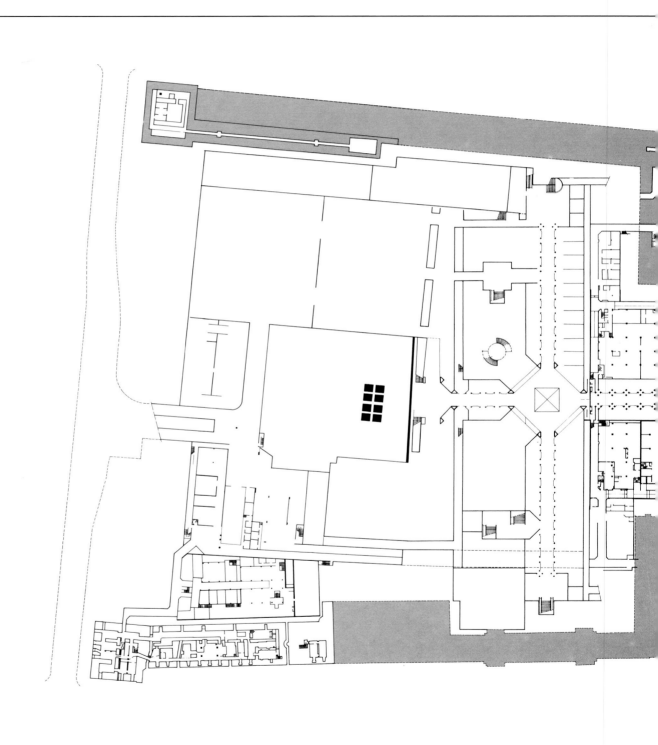

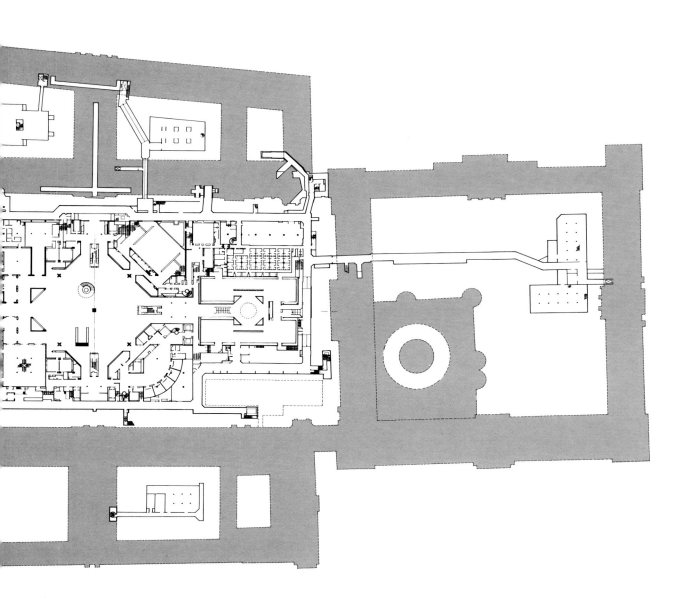

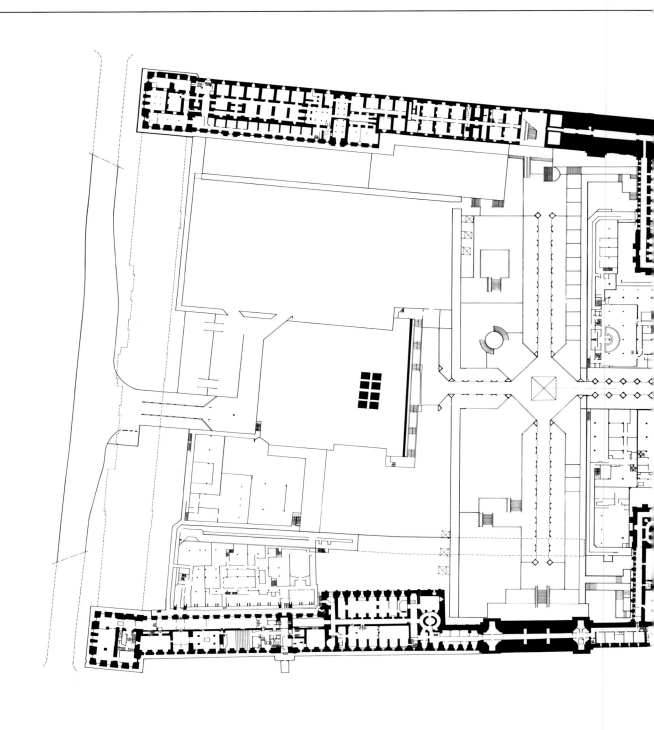

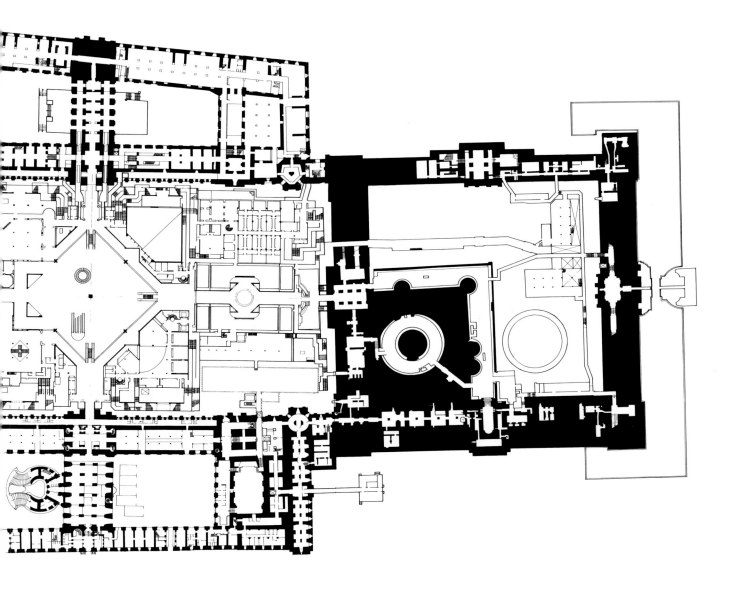

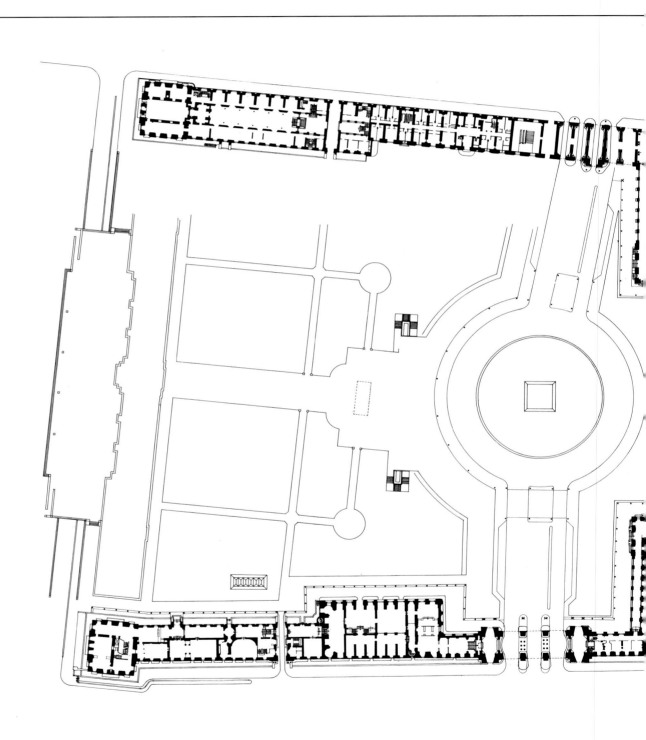

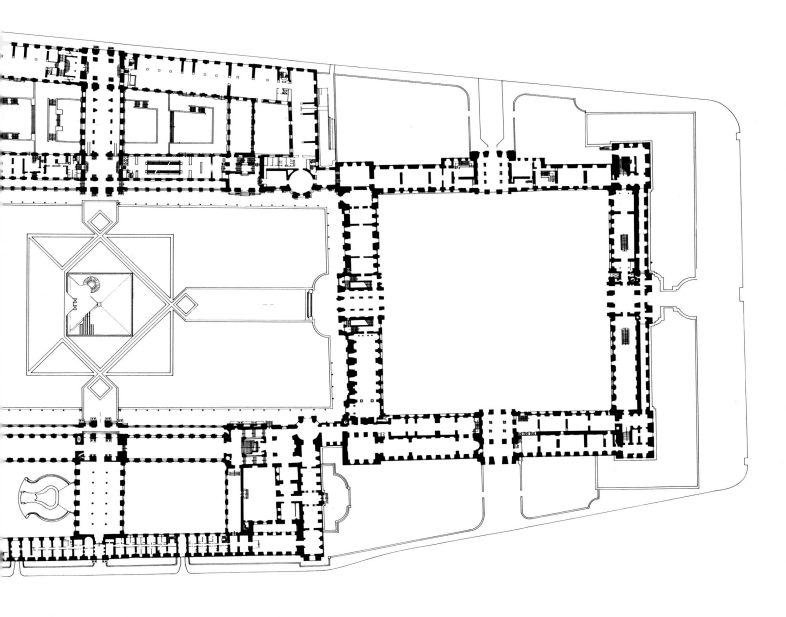

*The architectural forms compose geometric figures that are repeated right down to the very pattern of the paving slabs.*

## A TEAM DEDICATED TO A PROGRAM

Design work on the program of the Grand Louvre proceeded as the architects were honing the general scheme; the worked-up sketch – the interpretation of the program in spatial and architectural terms – was completed in July 1984. This dialogue between program designers, client body and architects during the preparatory phase was the essential prerequisite for an extremely straightforward general scheme, and for a program which kept to schedule to a remarkable degree.

In particular, the program for the reception area incorporated – in its worked-up version – basic features underpinning I.M. Pei's architecture; it was thus all the more appropriately suited to deal with the architectural constraints involved. Fundamentally, the scheme can be said to have reached a definitive stage by 1984. In other words, from this point on, design work for the provision of specific programs and their inter-relationship, along with design work on circulations and volumes, proceeded within the overall framework which had been set out by I.M. Pei.

Public reception facilities were logically distributed around the central space. Group reception, guided tours, the auditorium and temporary exhibitions room were installed in the east sector, on the museum side. The bookshop and restaurants were located opposite, in the west sector beside the carpark, tour coach park and Carrousel-Louvre shopping arcade. Finally, Louvre staff facilities were disposed in a circular arrangement and lay between the public facilities and the Louvre palace.

An absolute, pre-determined geometrical principle governed the entire design and building process; ostensibly the scheme which has been completed today corresponds to the very same scheme, the broad outlines of which had been sketched out by I.M. Pei in early 1984.

When I.M. Pei discusses his scheme, he starts out by speaking of the Louvre. Although he stresses the disparity between the various groups of buildings built in different architectural styles over the centuries, he emphasises the clear, coherent general arrangement of the present day ensemble, and the classicism and regularity of the façades by Pierre Lescot, Le Vau, Perrault, Percier and Fontaine, Visconti and Lefuel.

He then goes on to express his concern to preserve this unity and coherence by drawing inspiration from what he calls the ''French spirit'', with its characteristic blend of logic and geometry.

The pyramid, which has been the object of so much debate and controversy, forms the entrance to the museum. Although it has to appear as a landmark, the architect wants it to be transparent, so that it will contribute to reinforcing the presence of the Louvre and to highlighting the major features of the palace architecture.

Its form, dimensions, and the design of its accompanying basins have been strictly governed

by the axes and the proportioning of the courtyard and of the surrounding buildings, exactly in keeping with the French spirit to which I.M. Pei refers. He then proceeds to establish a straightforward relationship between this surface composition and the basement areas.

The level of the public reception beneath the pyramid is situated at −9 m, in order to open up the volumes to the greatest extent possible: the pyramid infuses the space with daylight, thus eliminating any impression one might have of being buried. The change in level between the reception area and the museum has been reduced by the introduction of a mezzanine floor which is linked to the lower floors of the museum.

With its straightforward forms and harmonious volumes, and the rational manner in which links were provided and the various functions within the program installed, the scheme possessed an impregnable strength and consistency.

Whereas the dominant feature of the architecture is extreme clarity, an extreme complexity, on the other hand, characterizes the constant desire to organize the component features in a rational and aesthetic manner; this can be seen in the coordination of technical facilities and in the pursuit of solutions which often explore the very limits of state-of-the-art technology.

The sole technical features which have been left exposed in this architecture of architectonic concrete and stone (lighting systems, air intakes, cameras, smoke-detectors etc.) add to the coherence of line and form, and provide emphasis and punctuation without ever creating any jarring effect. A remarkable application has gone into integrating the power cables, air and smoke-extraction ducts, air-conditioning, water supply and plumbing. Indeed, a determined quest for co-ordination and synthesis was required in order to harmonize all these components, and to see to it that they could be accommodated in the girders and concrete slabs, in the forms stipulated by the architect.

I.M. Pei is a demanding architect; he gets what he wants without showing impatience or having to autocratically impose his views. He merely has a force of conviction or, rather, he leaves his architecture to speak for him and to vindicate his choice. Architects, engineers, contractors, master craftsmen, and workers, all brought the best of their talents and skills to bear in the course of the undertaking. In this respect, the Pei team proved to be a challenging partner for the client body which was preoccupied by the program, the financial provision and the deadlines.

If I.M. Pei has referred to the French spirit in

order to vindicate his scheme, what has come across – persistently, patiently, and without the slightest complacency or compromise – has been the driving spirit of I.M.Pei himself and of all his team. The accomplishment of this work, however, also witnessed an assertion of French *savoir faire,* and the result deserves respect and admiration.

This team work – involving the archaeologists who revealed the marvelous vestiges, the designers who managed to integrate these into their project, and the contractors who executed the designs so well – will now be examined. We shall begin with the cour Carrée, then go on to the cour Napoléon and the Richelieu wing, and, finally, consider the famous pyramid itself.

Above
*The pyramid lit up at night with the diamond mesh of the glazed panels and the load bearing structure transparently visible.*

Opposite
*The spiral staircase down to the reception level; in the center of the staircase, the platform elevator for disabled visitors.*

Above
*Pottery from groups
of buildings closed off
in the 14th century
and in 1528.*

Opposite
*Charles VI's helmet
reconstructed from
fragments found
in the well in
the Philippe Auguste keep.*

## THE COUR CARRÉE

In 1528, when François I decided to demolish the large tower of Philippe Auguste's old Louvre and to fill in the moats, little could he have imagined that, almost five centuries later, the ramparts of the fortress would once again be revealed and cleared, and then highlighted in testimony to a place which was the cradle of the French kingdom. Indeed, the relics discovered were extensive, and comprised vestiges of the two north and east wings of Philippe Auguste's fortified castle and of its central keep.

### The excavations

The moats of the fortress were completely cleared, revealing the mighty counterscarp wall, and bases of the main parts of the building and of the defensive towers; striking features such as the tour du Milieu, the tour de la Taillerie – gate-towers over the east gate and the draw-bridge pier – were further interesting highlights of this fortress which had been built outside the city walls, on a site commanding the Seine as it flowed into Paris.

A tunnel was driven between the moats and the ditch around the keep: this afforded a view of the remains of the impressive base under the Louvre's large tower. In addition to this remarkably well preserved architectural feature, the substructure of Charles V's castle – built on the foundations of the fortress and overhanging the ditch surrounding the keep – is also visible. The way in which the stonework in this building has been dressed, the quality of the pointing, and the regular bondings are all features which illustrate how the art of building had evolved over the centuries.

A second tunnel was dug in order to link the ditch surrounding the keep with the basement of the Louvre in the west section of the mediaeval palace, above which – during the reigns of François I and Henri II – the Renaissance wing of the cour Carrée and the salle des Cariatides had been built. The remains of a Gothic room, built in the reign of Saint-Louis (including columns, capitals, and the bases of the original vaulted arches) have also been uncovered here.

Together, these features make up an archaeological circuit covering the period from Philippe Auguste to Charles V.

This circuit has been integrated into the museum circuits by means of the links to the cour Napoléon provided under the Sully pavilion, and to the museum under the Arts pavilion; access to the Egyptian and Greco-Roman Antiquities has also been provided.

There is a striking transition from the modernism of I.M. Pei's reception area to the mediaeval vestiges. The unveiling of the defensive walls revealed the first link in a historical chain which stretches over eight centuries.

The excavations carried out by Berty in 1866 had enabled measured drawings to be made of the upper layers of masonrywork buried under the

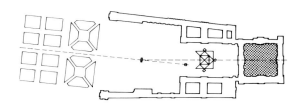

cour Carrée. Berty, however, confined himself to a superficial exploration.

In late 1983, Michel Fleury – in collaboration with Venceslas Kruta – was commissioned with the new excavation works. For a year, the teams of archaeologists removed the material which filled the moats, wells, tanks and cellars within the area delimited by the foundations of the old Louvre. Although the excavations were completed in one year, research work is still continuing, as the spoil removed from the site was stored prior to being thoroughly examined – an operation which will still require much time.

Nevertheless, a number of fascinating discoveries have already been made. A series of vases dating from before 1360, as well as numerous artefacts (pottery, bottles, sundry objects, glasses, stoneware) were discovered in the latrines and at the bottom of the moats, in the lower layer of the fill; the latter area was of particular interest because it contained samples which ante-dated the filling in of the moats. A number of remarkable finds were made in the well of the keep:

– two small pennants bearing the emblem of Charles VI;

– fragments of a copper crown worn by Charles VI on his helmet; fragments of the helmet itself; and a medallion bearing the arms of the Dauphin Louis.

These various objects – all indisputably of royal ownership – had probably been thrown into the well by a thief who, believing them to be gold, had broken them in order to melt them down; on discovering that they were were not gold he must have thrown them away in frustration, or perhaps out of mere prudence.

### The layout of the archaeological spaces

The archaeological vestiges of the old Louvre have been protected by a reinforced concrete slab covering the walls and moats, and forming the ground level of the cour Carrée which was subsequently paved. However, as it was not safe to bring weight to bear on the old masonrywork without the risk of damage, the slab is not supported by the vestiges themselves, but rests on piles which have been built *in situ*, or sunk down to the limestone bed, behind the old masonrywork.

M. Duval, Head Palace Architect, resolutely adopted a straightforward, unambiguous architectural treatment. He retained the untreated concrete aspect of the elements which cover the moats and house the vestiges. The areas where the stone facing of the walls had crumbled away were packed in order to strengthen the entire structure; the packing was set back from the existing stone facing, leaving the vestiges in the condition they were in when they were discovered. The bottom of the outer ditches was reinforced by means of a raft which abutted the wall bases. On the other hand, the original paving in the ditch surrounding the keep was retained and painstakingly restored. Networks of ventilation, air-conditioning, and smoke-

extraction ducts were incorporated either in the raft, or under the surface of the cour Carrée.

The presence of the old Louvre with its towers and counterscarp walls creates a remarkably evocative impression. It was also necessary, however, to provide public circulation spaces with resistant flooring material. Stone was rejected as it would have been misleading from a strictly archaeological point of view : the original moats had been filled with water and had not been floored. The architects D. Brard and J. Alonso finally opted for a wooden footbridge which was built slightly clear of the bottom of the moat. The footbridge features a straightforward design of close-fitting stout planks, and runs well clear of the vestiges, parallel to the counterscarp walls; it has been

Top
*The moat of*
*Philippe Auguste's fortress,*
*henceforth open to the public:*
*the towers on*
*the Cité entrance side,*
*and the draw bridge pier.*

Above
*In the background:*
*the sphinx crypt*
*through which visitors*
*can enter the museum;*
*this entrance was pierced*
*through the palace*
*foundations.*

*The Marengo porch.*
*The cambered courtyard*
*and the lip of the central*
*basin are visible.*

Right hand page
*The Saint-Germain*
*l'Auxerrois porch.*

widened at three points, so that visitors can pause to admire the most striking features in the circuit.

The architecture of the fortress has been highlighted by means of variable-intensity adjustable spotlights mounted the entire length of the ramparts on a track suspended from the roof of the crypts.

### The treatment of the ground level

Architecture was an integral feature of the scheme for the layout of the ground level within the cour Carrée; this scheme was inspired by a Second Empire project drawn up by Duban, who had planned to build a circular fountain basin in the middle of the courtyard. The archaeological excavations, moreover, revealed traces of the original foundations for this fountain; the Emperor, however, had disliked the project, and it had been abandoned.

The courtyard is slightly convex, a feature which has met with criticism from some parts. In fact, this convexity meets two requirements: it provides maximum headroom in the basement for the vestiges; it furthermore leaves the base of the palace façades unobstructed.

The courtyard is paved with cobblestones: the overall area has been divided into four paved sections separated by alleys that have been treated with larger granite paving stones; these alleys un from the pavilions and link up around the fountain.

### The restoration of the palace

The Grand Louvre project naturally focussed around the museum and the related scientific programs; the project could not, however, be carried out without the restoration of the palace in which it was to be accommodated.

The buildings were in a critical state of delapidation and decay. The roofs leaked, the lead decorative ornamentation on the pavilions was badly eroded and was in danger of falling off. The statues, the carving on the chimneys, and the stonework of the façades were all in a similarly advanced state of decomposition, and in some instances had actually disappeared. Although the task was colossal, it was fundamental to the conservation of the national patrimony. The undertaking cost more than a billion francs.

The palace restoration operation began with the cour Carrée. For a whole year, the façades were concealed behind a huge scaffolding, and a corrugated metal canopy covered the roofs. Forty eight firms of contractors worked on the roofs; they restored the chimneys, deepened the gutters that were too shallow for the snow, entirely replaced faulty roof timbers and roofing slates, and built identical reproductions of the lead decorative features on the pavilions. Such works called for skilled stone masons, and for specialized craftsmen to restore the lead roof features using specially resculpted wooden forms. Faulty masonrywork was restored on the façades before the traditional cleaning operation was carried out: more than 300 m³ of stones were removed and sculpted *in situ* by thirty master masons who replaced the capitals, garlands, finials, consoles and figures. Finally, metal frames and 20 mm thick burglar-proof panes were fitted to the windows as a security measure.

This massive undertaking, however, represents less than 10% of the total restoration work on the Louvre palace; restoration is gradually continuing as the renovation works proceed on the museum and its immediate vicinity.

Until now, exhibits had rarely been displayed on the third floor of the cour Carrée, as the Department of Paintings only occupied the half of the south wing on the cour Carrée side (the other half, on the Seine side, accommodated offices for the curators and the administration) and the west half-wing to the south of the Sully pavilion, i.e. 1 800 m² out of the 7 670 m² on the third floor. The remaining area accommodated various museum departments (restoration, reserve storerooms etc.)

The extension of the project to the entire floor area on the third floor has begun. The architect Italo Rota – working in collaboration with the Set-Foulquier technical design office – has been commissioned with the layout of the east, south and west wings. Compared with the project for the north wing – begun in 1981 – the new provisions for toplighting include systems which allow the amount of natural lighting to be adapted to seasonal weather conditions.

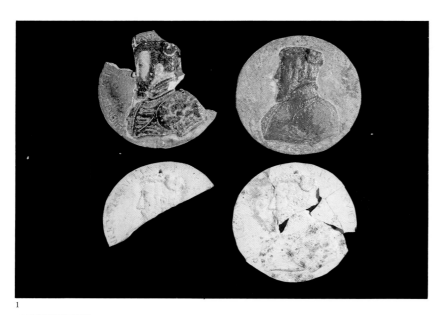

1

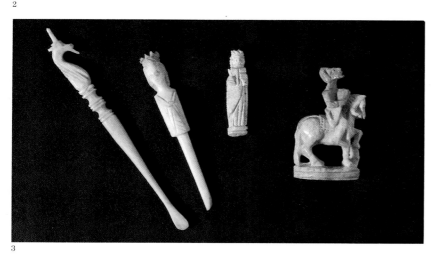

2

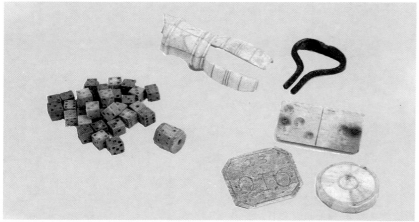

3

4

5

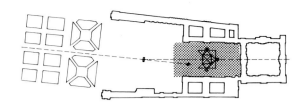

## THE COUR NAPOLÉON

### The excavations

In late 1983, Yves de Kisch, Inspector General of Archaeology and Director of Historical Antiquities for the Ile-de-France region, was commissioned with the archaeological excavations in the cour Napoléon and the place du Carrousel. This was the largest archaeological undertaking ever carried out in France. For two years, more than eighty archaeologists and technicians explored a site of about three hectares, helped by forty workmen and some thirty youngsters on Government Youth Training Schemes, and a further twenty volunteers. Pierre-Jean Trombetta was in the charge of the excavation site.

An intelligible topographical picture of these five hectares of Paris has emerged as a result of the archival research conducted, and the work carried out on site.

Until Philippe Auguste had a wall built within the alluvial flood zone, the area was rural. It had been inhabited since neolithic times (4000 BC) – remains of dwellings and sepultures indicate the presence of some of the earliest known farmers in the Ile-de-France region. Throughout the site, remains of enclosures, numerous graves, and a small cemetry, point to fairly intensive farming activity in the Gallic period. There are a few traces of episodic inhabitation, both in the Gallo-Roman period and the Middle Ages (6th-9th centuries): the numerous remains discovered (ditches, graves, furrows, sepultures) bear witness to farming activity, and to the presence of a nearby village – probably located near the banks of the Seine. For the following three centuries, no trace of occupation has been found.

A new lease of activity came about with the building of Philippe Auguste's fortress and the city ramparts. The area became a *faubourg*, or inner suburb, taking on a form it was to retain up until the 18th century. The Royal menagerie, kitchens, and other palace facilities were built near the Louvre. One particular archaeological find revealed a midden containing bones from the Royal falconry (eagles, gyrfalcons and peregrine falcons) dating from around the mid 14th century.

It was here that, in the mid 17th century, Louis Le Vau began the works which were to give the palace architectural unity and, in time, link it to the Tuileries château. These works had gone no further than an initial phase, evidence of which was brought to light in the course of the excavations: a moat – matching the other moat on the east side of the cour Carrée which André Malraux had had cleared and restored. The counterscarp wall of this moat has been integrated into the future archaeological circuit.

Beyond this, an urban fabric had developed to the east and west of the rue Fromenteau. Even before the period which yielded most archaeological evidence (from the 13th to the 18th centuries),

houses had been built there. The original inhabitants of the rue Fromenteau were artisans and tradesmen and, despite the building of aristocratic town houses, and the proximity of the palace and of the Saint-Thomas church, the street long remained the part of the neighbourhood where ordinary Parisian people lived.

The extensive rebuilding that was carried out always followed the layout of the old parcels; there are hundreds of archaeological features (cellars, cess-pools, wells and ovens) which enable an accurate picture to be drawn up of the area, its inhabitants, and their way of life.

Up till the 16th century, the central zone of the cour Napoléon – which extended to the rampart west of the rue Saint-Thomas-du-Louvre – still had a semi-rural aspect (vegetable gardens, and other plots under cultivation); numerous archaeological traces of this have been discovered (lines of holes dug for fence-posts, pits). The area was transformed during the classic period when large town houses – notably the hôtel de Chevreuse-Longueville – were erected.

Beyond the Charles V rampart lay a sizeable neighbourhood in which artisan and craft activities flourished. The excavations carried out under the site of the future *musées de France* laboratory and museum service facilities revealed an impressive battery of tile-kilns, dating back to the 15th and 16th centuries (where Bernard Palissy may have worked), and a series of related buildings.

Exploration work was also carried out on the site of the former château des Tuileries, but few interesting vestiges were discovered. Here, the ground floor level had stood higher than the present-day level, and, apart from vestiges of the substructure of the 17th century theatre to the north, the remaining walls formed part of basements which were of little archaeological interest.

Between March 1986 and December 1987, a team of some twenty archaeologists and technicians began a careful examination of these various finds. Objects were categorized, documents cleaned up, and the archaeological evidence carefully sifted and analysed; this has already resulted in the publication of several specialised articles in scholarly reviews. Moreover, a number of manuscripts concerning the pre-urban, mediaeval and modern periods, along with extensive series of artefacts (pottery, glassware), are already available for research. Finally, the *Institut français d'architecture* organized an exhibition in which the general topography of the area was presented; furthermore, the 1989 National Exhibition to be staged in the Grand Palais – "Thirty Years of Archaeology in France" – will devote considerable importance to the excavations carried out in the cour Napoléon.

The start of works on the second phase of the Grand Louvre project – involving the building of the carparks and the Carrousel-Tuileries shopping arcade – will signal the launch of a further round

1. Four stages
in the making
of a Bernard Palissy
terracotta medallion
depicting Henri II.

2. Gaming
and musical objects
found in a well.

3. Everday ivory objects;
left: a toilet implement
in the shape
of a mediaeval unicorn ;
right: top of
a 17th century spoon handle
featuring a monkey
mounted on a horse.

4. Late 17th century
terracotta model
from a sculptor's studio
in the former
rue Fromenteau.

5. Avon potteryware
(school of Bernard Palissy).

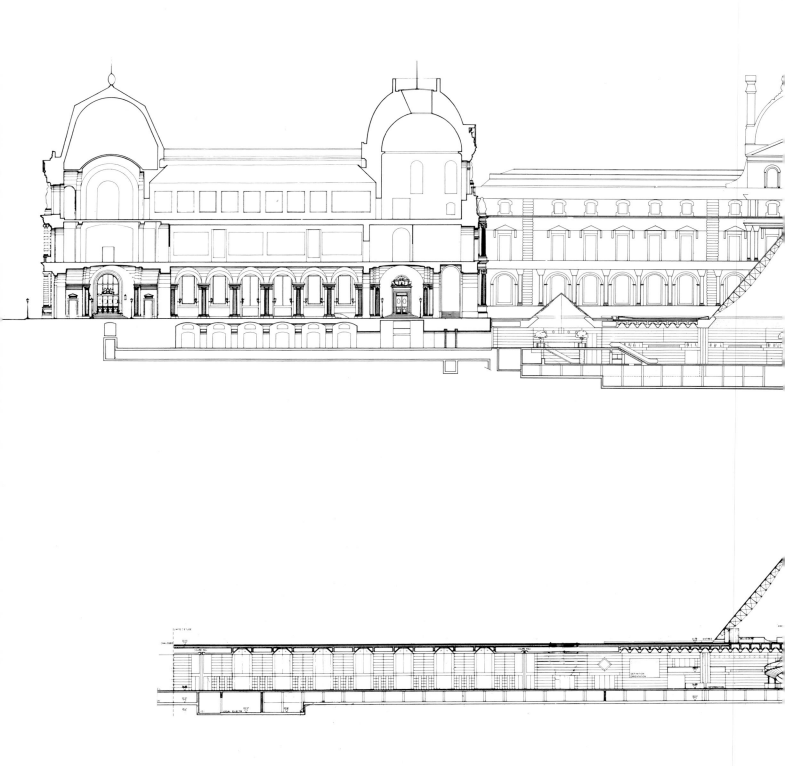

110

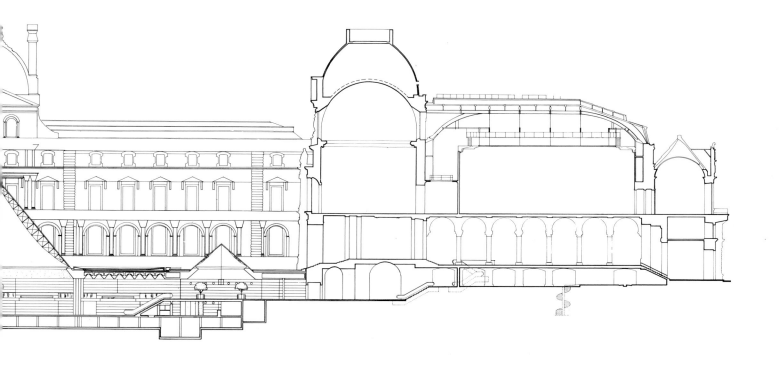

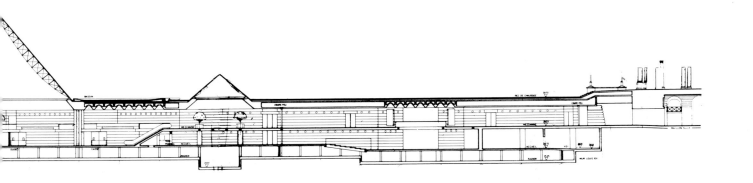

111

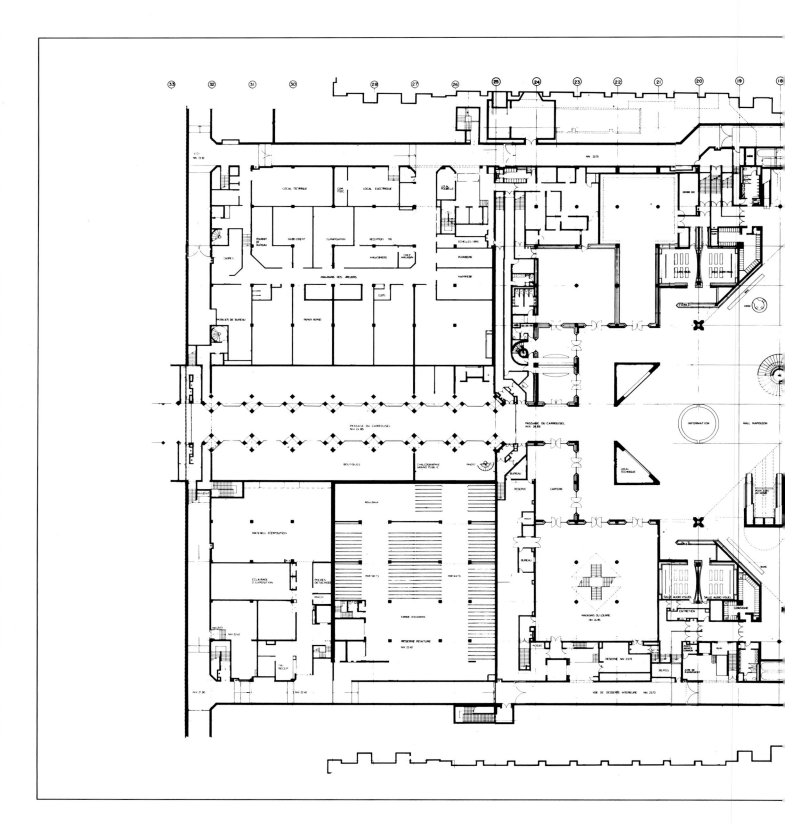

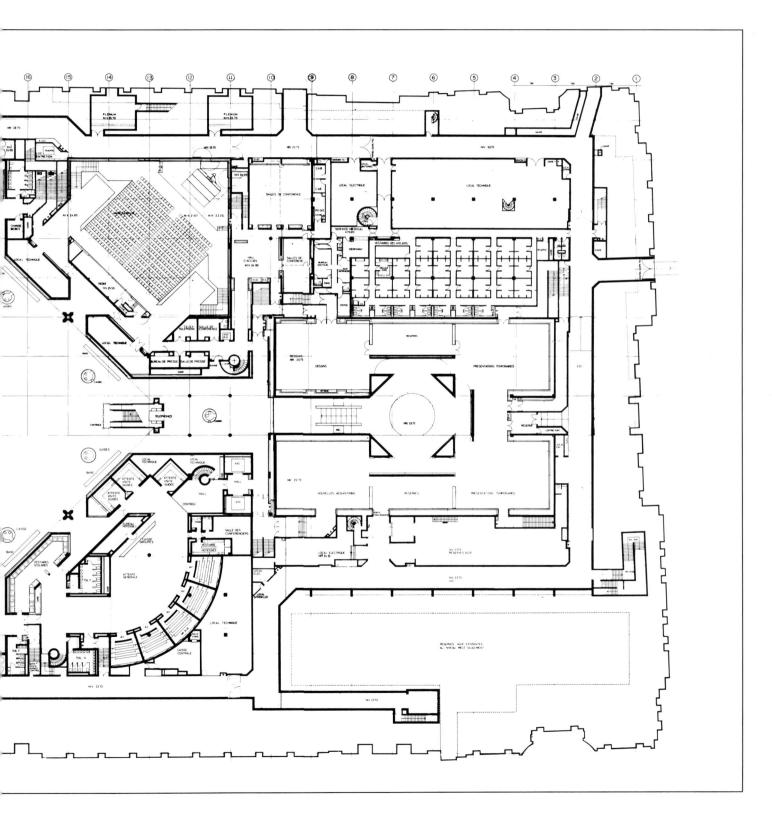

113

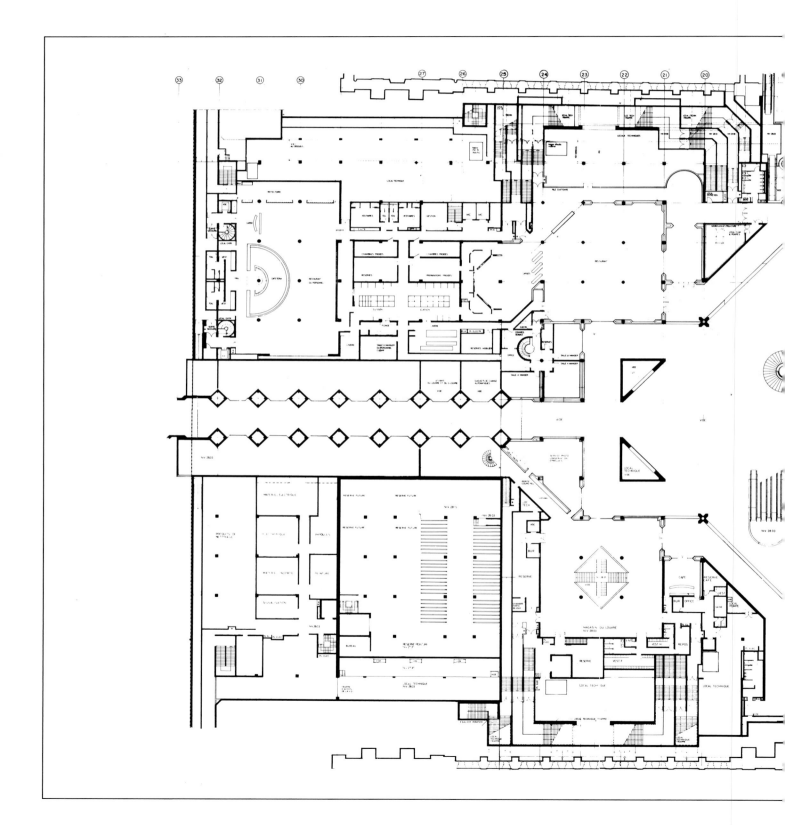

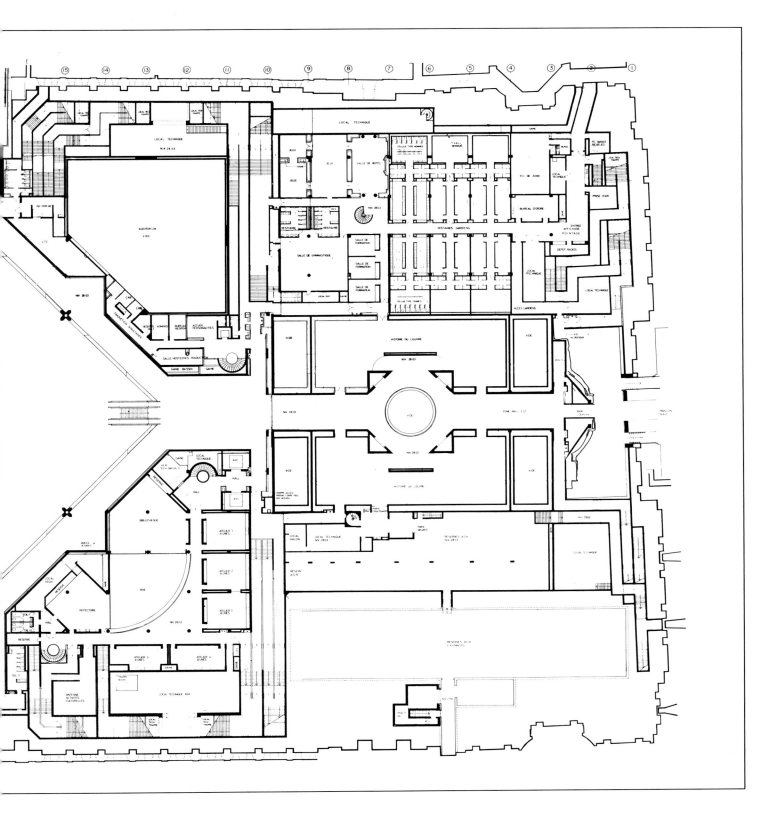

115

*1. View from the mezzanine of the spiral staircase leading to the reception beneath the pyramid.*

*2. Entrance to the museum restaurants.*

*3. The ticket office on the Richelieu wing side.*

*4. View through one of the windows in the museum cafeteria. In the background, the museum bookshop.*

of archaeological excavations, over an area of some 30 000 m².

Although available evidence from the trial bores already carried out, and from the works on the provision of a museum laboratory and delivery area being undertaken in the south part of this sector has indicated that this area will probably yield fewer vestiges than the others already explored, the new round of excavations will allow investigation of :
 – further traces of neolithic and Gallic habitats;
 – the tile workshops;
 – the relics of the counterscarp of the Charles V rampart, part of which could, furthermore, be included in the new scheme.

### The treatment of the basement spaces

The cour Napoléon forms the hub of the new museum sequence, and is basically given over to public reception, and to vital museum staff and storage facilities. These facilities are entirely laid out below ground and occupy the whole floor area to a depth of − 14 m on three levels.

#### 1. The technical floor

This is located on the lowest level and provides the supply of wet services, water, air, and the medium and low voltage power required by each program. The premises are also used for the transit and distribution of ventilation and smoke-extraction ducts, and house the air-handling unit, the power transformer stations, and the smoke-extraction plant. Thus, as new needs arise, or as more advanced technology becomes available, it will be possible to eventually supplement or modify the various supply systems without interfering directly in the areas concerned or obstructing the normal running of the museum. The technical premises have straightforward circulations and a pleasant work environment. They also house the main security facilities which are entirely run by the museum.

#### 2. The reception

The reception level covers the entire floor area of the volume that has been excavated to a depth of − 9 m from ground level, except for a zone located between the pyramid and the cour Carrée, where the level was lowered to − 10 m in order to provide extra headroom for the temporary exhibition rooms. It includes the following programs:

The centrally located reception space itself; this consists of a vast 53 m square room, located in the center of the cour Napoléon and lying at a 45° angle to the axes of the Denon, Richelieu and Sully pavilions. Various related departments and programs are distributed around this square on the same level. Visitors can enter in three different ways:
 – from ground level under the pyramid; two escalators, a staircase and a elevator provide a link with the entrance belvedere;
 – via the Richelieu arcade which runs between the rue de Rivoli and the cour Napoléon; two banks

1

3

116

2

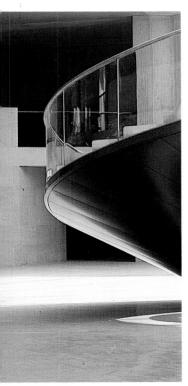

4

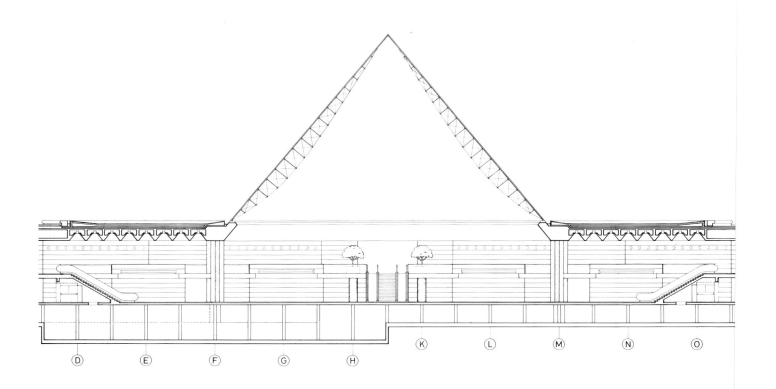

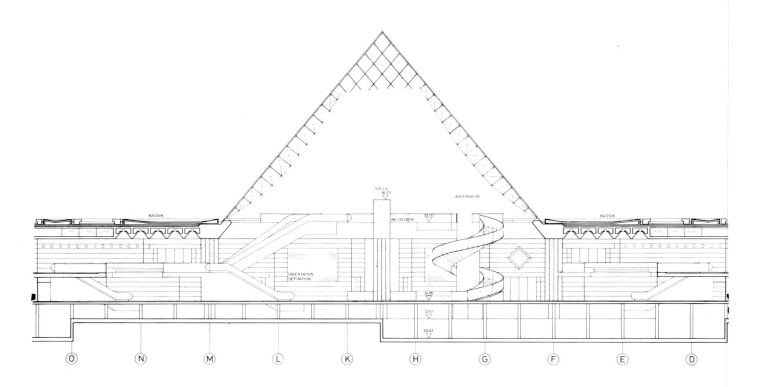

# THE ARCHITECTONIC CONCRETE

In the architectural treatment, concrete has been used as a noble material on equal terms with stone, glass or stainless steel. The plastic properties, appearance and color of the concrete make it a feature of the highest quality; the visitor even has difficulty in distinguishing between the stone and the concrete, such is the degree of uniformity in color and texture between the two materials.

Although the composition of the concrete and the finishing of the facing are highly sophisticated, the forms themselves are, on the other hand, quite straightforward. I.M. Pei was fully aware that concrete touches up badly and that, consequently, the process of release from mould has to be flawless. The angles of the planes were specially designed to facilitate the delicate yet vital task of removing the shuttering and to avoid spalling effects. In general, demanding standards of concrete construction and execution were pursued and achieved.

To begin with, in order to obtain a precise idea of the goal to be attained, the contractor was invited to visit the Fine Arts Museum in Boston and the National Gallery in Washington along with the construction site managers: the Dumez corporation was presented with a sort of challenge.

Then, a mock up of a large section of one of the structures enabled constructional details to be worked out in a full scale simulation. During this phase, decisions were taken concerning the final choice of timber to be used in formwork, the treatment to be applied to the wooden boards, the exact composition of the concrete to be poured, and precise details concerning the construction and shape of the shuttering. Jean-Pierre Aury, the French architectonic concrete specialist, was consulted for the choice of the precise composition of the concrete and the finishing treatments.

## The formwork

The shuttering used for the sections of architectonic concrete that would eventually be visible was lined with a layer of close-grained knotless Oregon pine battens; these were 53 mm wide, 16 mm thick and were sawn along the grain. The boards were dried to bring the level of moisture content down to 12%, before being planed smooth. Once assembled, the layer of boards was damp-proofed and heat-proofed using resin. Before pouring began, all the formwork components had been treated with a white cement laitance that was then cleaned and sandpapered.

While in place, the shuttering was protected from bad weather. The site workers wore slippers, and the forms were protected by plastic sheets before the reinforcement bars were installed. The reinforcement components were suspended from scaffolding to avoid all direct contact with the formwork. The forms were vacuum-cleaned before the concrete was finally poured.

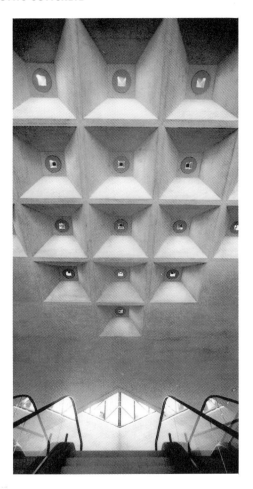

The lighting in the architectonic concrete honeycomb ceiling has been integrated into the air-extractor vents.

## The surface

Despite the meticulous care taken in the construction and preparation of the formwork, and in the actual pouring in the concrete, a number of stains appeared when the shuttering was removed. Two further courses of treatment were therefore applied: the first consisted in scrubbing the exposed surfaces with a solution of water and diluted acid; the second, in sandblasting and giving a smooth finish. The architectonic surfaces that can be seen today are a testimony to the successful way in which architects and contractor combined efforts.

As a result, the concrete is barely distinguishable from the stonework that features in the wall facings and the flooring. Magny stone has been used for the walls, while the flooring has been treated with more resistant Chassagne stone ; both blend harmoniously with the color of the existing stonework of the palace façades.

of escalators have been provided and these lead to the north corner of the square;

– via the basement; a gallery links the west corner of the square to the carparks and coach park laid out under the Carrousel gardens.

Public facilities and services have been provided around the four sides of the square; these consist, successively, of:

– a large 1 300 m² twin level shop to the rear of the south-west side of the square. This comprises a large art bookshop, a print shop selling reproductions of engravings on display in the Louvre, a shop selling casts and jewelry, and a postcard shop;

– a twin level restaurant complex on the north-west side. This comprises a *brasserie* and a café on the reception level, and a public restaurant and staff restaurant on the upper level;

– an auditorium and three conference rooms on two levels on the north-east side. The auditorium has 429 seats; one of the conference rooms has accommodation for 80 people, the other two can each seat 40 people;

– finally, on the south-east side – similarly laid out on two levels – spaces for group reception and for the organization of guided tours and lectures.

Three of the four upper corners of the square point towards the three museum entrances: Denon, Richelieu and Sully. Ticket and guide-book sales desks, cloakrooms, toilets and left-luggage facilities have been grouped together in these three zones. The west sector of the square is given over to public information.

The information bank has been installed under the belvedere. Two wall panels offer descriptions of the collections and the various masterpieces which can be seen in the three museum circuits, as well as details of current activities at the Louvre: temporary exhibitions, concerts, symposia, etc. TV monitors provide information on the works on display, and indicate which rooms are open or closed.

The entire range of facilities grouped around the central square under the pyramid function independently and outwith museum opening times. They are related to the current programs in the auditorium, the temporary exhibitions, and the museum's commercial activities. Although the museum runs and supervises the area under the pyramid, the public enjoys free access. The museum proper actually only begins on the mezzanine level.

### 3. The mezzanine

The latter extends like a balcony around the square, leaving the volume beneath the pyramid entirely unobstructed. The three main entrances to the museum are provided on this mezzanine which links up with the museum sequence via the basement levels of the Richelieu, Sully and Denon pavilions.

Unlike the reception space, the mezzanine spaces are supervised by the museum to which their functioning is directly related.

The bookshop, museum shops, public and staff restaurants are all installed in the west sector.

In the east sector are to be found the conference rooms connected to the auditorium, and the cultural activities rooms for young people.

Further along the route leading to the Sully pavilion are to be found two symmetrical spaces which house the "History of the Louvre" section – a permanent exhibition devoted to the history of the Louvre from the time of Philippe Auguste down to the present day. This program provides an introduction to the archaeological circuit through the moats of the Philippe Auguste fortress beneath the cour Carrée.

The various facilities for the museum staff are located separately, behind the public spaces. The cloakrooms, rest areas, gymnasia, workshop stores, and security and office premises are located to the north, whereas the Greco-Roman Antiquities and Painting reserves are found to the south. A 4×4 m service route (Vdi) runs round the entire courtyard, providing circulation for artworks and museum material; branches of this route also extend under the cour Carrée and the main buildings, serving the museum and exhibition rooms, and affording access to the reserves where the artworks are stored. This internal service route extends eastwards along the Flore wing to the delivery area which can handle trucks of all sizes and is itself linked to the avenue du Général-Lemonnier underpass.

### Links between the reception area and the palace

The mezzanine level is located more than 1 m below the levelling courses of the palace foundations. The provision of links with the palace therefore involved highly intricate works in the course of which the level of the Louvre's foundations had

*The escalators linking the belevedere located beneath the pyramid at ground level and the reception.*

*Left hand page*
*Top*
*The auditorium.*

*Bottom*
*One access from the reception to the mezzanine.*
*In the background, one of the three smaller pyramids that signal the direction of the three main museum entrances.*
*The color and appearance of the architectonic concrete ceiling and of the stone walls are remarkably similar.*

to be lowered, and openings pierced through the bases of the façades.

Special precautions were taken to extricate the solid foundations bearing the massive weight of the pavilion superstructures. The solution consisted in injecting a mixture of cement and silicate gel into the sand upon which the palace lay, and then constructing piles by means of a jet-grouting process involving the high-speed injection of cement under a pressure of 400 bars in order to replace the existing subsoil. Once these reinforcement works were completed, the foundations could be cleared and partially deepened.

The most delicate operation proved to be the piercing through of the west base wall of the Sully pavilion. Rather than forming a single building, this pavilion is actually made up of three successive façades: the Renaissance façade, the Louis XIV façade, and the Napoleon III façade; these had been built in turn, and merely abutted one another rather than being joined together. It was impossible to pierce through any one of the three base walls without running the risk of creating a ''wedge'' effect which would shift the load and thus destabilize the entire pavilion. The solution adopted consisted in carrying out reinforcement works on the three walls, prior to piercing through them; as earth-moving work progressed, successive layers of stainless steel bars were sealed horizontally into the masonrywork and anchored to solid blocks of reinforced concrete on either side. This allowed the works to be carried out without resorting to special shoring procedures.

This whole intricate process meant that protective measures had to be taken, and that the effects on the building in the course of the works had to be accurately monitored. Careful inspection and auscultation of the building was therefore carried out in order to check for any eventual movement. This operation was conducted by the *Bureau des recherches géologiques et minières*, Brgm (Office of Geological and Mining Research); it enabled all movements to be accurately monitored, and the reinforcement works on the foundations to be adjusted in correlation with the data obtained.

### The ground level layouts

The cour Napoléon extends throughout the central zone of the Louvre within the limits of that part of the palace built under Napoleon III.

The center of the courtyard is henceforth occupied by the glass pyramid. The triangular belvedere of the pyramid provides access to the reception space to which it is linked by twin escalators and a spiral staircase; a special elevator for the disabled has been installed in the newel of the staircase.

The pyramid is surrounded by triangular basins, the shapes of which correspond exactly to the geometry of the reception space ; this design is a reference to Le Nôtre's original design for flower beds in the Tuileries gardens – a design which

I.M.Pei wishes to re-create in place of the layout of the existing gardens – known as *jardins réservés* (and which lie between the avenue du Général-Lemmonier and the present day gates to the Tuileries).

Three small glass pyramids are located in front of the north, east and south basins, over the staircases which lead from the reception area to the mezzanine level and hence to the museum itself. By the positions in which they are placed, and because of their transparent appearance, in relationship to the palace, they serve as markers directing the visitors en route from the reception area.

The open space in front of the entrance to the pyramid, as well as the alleys leading from the small pyramids to the Richelieu, Sully and Denon pavilions, are paved with large slabs of black granite. The perimeter of the square has been treated in sandstone paving and features traditional Napoleon III designs.

Lighting in the square is provided by Napoleon III lamp-posts (either restored originals or faithful copies) which are positioned at regular intervals. The lanterns are equipped with low pressure fluorescent lamps, while the palace façades are lit by quartz halogen floodlights. Small granite posts provide additional lighting along the routes on either side of the main alley leading to the cour Carrée. The fountains in their basins, and the illuminated pyramid are additional features that contribute to the atmosphere of the lighting in the square.

Six small and two large triangular basins are laid out geometrically around the pyramid.

The edges of these basins have been treated in large blocks of black granite. The water comes to within a few centimetres of the edge, and is contained by polished black granite slabs forming a spillway. This creates the impression of water lapping the very edge of the basin.

Each of the large basins has two centrally located fountain jets; the height and diameter of the jets are adjustable, and the column of water can be as wide as 3 m and as high as 10 m, thus creating dancing water effects.

The treatment of the basins gave I.M. Pei the opportunity to demonstrate his skillful mastery of working with stone. The surrounding blocks of black granite bestow a classic monumental appearance upon the overall composition, and invite visitors to sit along the edges of the basins. The pyramid is highlighted in the multiple reflections that can be seen in the water.

The layout of the square – emphasizing the axes of the cour Napoléon – clearly indicates the fact that the pyramid is not aligned with the major perspective running between La Défense and the Carrousel, via the Etoile and the Champs-Elysées.

The pyramid is definitely out of line with the major axis. So, however, is the Sully pavilion, and no one is surprised. The reason for this lies in the construction of the palace itself: it is built on the banks of the Seine at a point where the river bends. Originally, the Tuileries palace completed the com-

position and concealed the fact that the composition was off-centre, but when the Tuileries disappeared, this became immediately apparent.

In order to assert this off-centre location, and to make quite clear that it is not the result of any error, the culminating point of the triumphal axis has been pin-pointed by a large equestrian statue of Louis XIV; this is a lead copy of the Bernini marble statue standing at Versailles[1].

The statue was made in the Coubertin founderies from a plastic cast taken by the sculptor M. Bourbon. Lead casting is a traditional craft technique; it involves creating a form made out of a sand and resin mixture poured over plaster copies cast in plastic moulds, along with a similarly made counter-form. A 10 mm layer of lead is then poured into the interstice between the form and counter-form. The various parts of the statue – head, legs etc. – are cast separately before being assembled together on a stout stainless steel structure; this provides a solid frame for the lead which would otherwise collapse under its own weight. The various parts of the sculpture are then welded together. The piece weighs seven tons: six tons of lead, and one ton of steel.

*The Bernini statue of Louis XIV and the fountain basins are features in the open court around the pyramid.*

1. Not only does the statue – with its forceful, dynamic form – fit perfectly into the overall composition, but it was sculpted by Bernini who – it should be recalled – had been commissioned by Louis XIV to complete the Louvre, although his projects had never been realized. The statue is thus a tribute to the memory of the sculptor. As for Louis XIV, everybody is aware of the major contribution which the king made to the Louvre palace; moreover, the statue of the monarch stands pointing in the direction his birthplace in Saint-Germain.

## VITAL URBANISTIC CONSIDERATIONS

The Louvre extends more than 700 m between the Seine and the rue de Rivoli, creating a kind of barrier between the city and the river. Moreover, the museum is tucked away – completely hidden behind the austere façades of the Ministry of Finance that run along the rue de Rivoli. The congested traffic in the latter street, and around the entrances to the *guichets* du Carrousel, forms an additional cordon between the palace from the city. It is hardly surprising that the cour Napoléon – completely cut off in this way – was gradually converted into a carpark for ministry and museum staff and also occasionally used as a parking facility for visitors.

No real parking facilities had been provided for the growing number of tour coaches, and the solutions which were hastily improvised proved disastrous. Access was rendered even more difficult by the double, even triple, rows of coaches permanently parked along the quays on the right bank of the Seine.

A similar situation prevailed in the rue de Rivoli, where there were the added complications of traffic, traffic jams and pollution.

The direction of traffic flow along the quays and in the rue de Rivoli meant that parking was on the left, and that visitors had to get out of the coaches onto the road, where there was a danger of being knocked down by traffic.

The situation was deplorable for the museum, visitors and Parisians alike, and was the object of a concerted move by public authorities to ensure that such difficulties would be taken into consideration with a view to finding an overall solution once the Grand Louvre project got underway.

The architects studied the question in collaboration with traffic experts from the City of Paris and the Prefecture of Police; the outcome was an overall scheme which focussed on four basic points:

### 1. Car and coach parking

The problem of car and coach parking is to be solved by the provision of underground carparks for cars and coaches beneath the Carrousel gardens. Visitors will be able to reach the museum directly via an underground link between these facilities and the Napoleon reception. This large complex – 600 parking places for cars, 80 parking bays for coaches – will allow traffic to be decongested in the vicinity of the Louvre, the quays, the Rue de rivoli, and the place du Palais Royal.

### 2. Traffic flow in the vicinity of the Louvre

Traffic in the avenue du Général-Lemonnier now uses the underpass, and this has enabled the architects to design a coherent layout of the gardens between Concorde and the arc de triomphe in the place du Carrousel. Moreover, the underpass provides access to the car and coach parking complex, and, at the same time, to the museum delivery area.

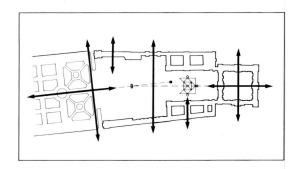

It was not possible to provide underground traffic flow in the place du Carrousel. With the Seine to the south, and Metro Line n° 1 running under the rue de Rivoli, it would only have been possible to create access ramps actually within the place du Carrousel, and the nature of the site itself ruled out such a solution. Moreover, building an underpass at this point would have meant inserting an obstacle between the car parks and coach park, and the Napoleon reception, and would have complicated liaison between the two areas.

Traffic in the place du Carrousel, therefore, was reduced. The south/north flow has been limited to taxis and buses; by reserving three of the four Rivoli *guichet* entrances for the north/south flow, traffic coming from the rue de Rivoli and the avenue de l'Opéra has been eased: this has de-obstructed the bottleneck at the Rivoli crossroads, and genuinely improved the situation in the place Colette.

### 3. The improvement of pedestrian routes and the creation of large public spaces

In this case, the decision to open up the Richelieu arcade between the place du Palais-Royal and the cour Napoléon enabled a new prestigious Paris public square to be created.

The normal Metro access to the museum has been changed. Henceforth, the nearest Metro to the museum is the twin Palais-Royal station, which is to be renamed "Palais-Royal/musée du Louvre". An additional *guichet* entrance has been reserved on the Rivoli side for pedestrians coming from the north-west (Rivoli-Opéra) direction, and this will help make the place du Carrousel more accessible.

### 4. The Carrousel-Louvre arcade

This shopping arcade is completely laid out underground, between the north and south *guichet* entrances to the place du Carrousel along a north/south mall; access from ground level is provided at either end of the mall near the *guichet* entrances to the Louvre.

This twin-level arcade intersects the east/west arcade running to the Napoleon reception, access to which is provided via a pedestrian subway; the subway comes out into the garden near the Arc de triomphe in the place du Carrousel. This ensemble is thus located between the tour coach park, the

car park and the Louvre. As a commercial amenity, it caters essentially for the museum visitors, but is also, in its own right, a lively attractive place which will lead to a better integration of the museum into city life.

Due to the proximity of the museum, the access spaces required a homogenous architectural treatment, the design of which has been entrusted to I.M. Pei. This has also entailed a specifically demanding choice as to the commercial activities which are to be developed within the precinct.

After the renovation of the Marais district, the building of the Pompidou Center and the newly-designed Les Halles area, the right bank of the Seine seemed to be outstripping the left; some even felt that the latter night fall into decline.

Within the Louvre museum, tucked away behind the austere façade of the palace, visitors could see the sculptures in the garden – the Marly horses and sculptures by Puget – through the large glazed bays of the Richelieu arcade. Their appetite thus whetted, they will want to visit the museum.

*The Cour Napoléon
towards the completion
of works.
It has become one
of the capital's choice
pedestrian squares.*

Left hand page
*General principles governing
pedestrian circulation
routes around
the Louvre palace.*

## THE RICHELIEU WING

This wing of the Louvre palace, running between the cour Carrée and the *guichet* entrances, was built under Napoleon III by the architects Visconti and Lefuel. Its interior is to be extensively re-designed. Since 1871, the wing has accommodated the administrative departments of the Ministry of Finance. These departments are to be re-located at Bercy in 1989, and their departure will allow conversion works on the building to begin.

The present wing comprises several main buildings distributed around three internal courtyards – the cour du Ministre to the west, and the cour des Caisses and cour de la Poste to the east.

The Richelieu arcade provides a ground floor link between the rue de Rivoli and the cour Napoléon, and also between the cour du Ministre and the cour des Caisses. On both the rue de Rivoli and cour Napoléon sides, the arcade terminates under two pavilions overlooking the adjacent buildings, aligned on the axis of the place du Palais-Royal.

The ground floor is slightly raised, and the general profile and proportioning of the façades highlights two upper levels of windows, one of which corresponds to the terrace overhanging the interior peristyle of the cour Napoléon. In most instances, however, although three main floors are visible from the exterior, the interior of the building actually features a "mezzanine treatment"; most of the interiors – apart from the State Rooms (The Duc de Morny Salon) and a few palatial rooms – have been laid out as office accommodation on five or six floors.

The mezzanine arrangement of these internal spaces is totally unsuited to the requirements of a museum layout. Ceiling heights are barely more than three or four meters, and the volumes are intersected by cross walls that house the countless chimney flues, the protruding stacks of which provide architectural cadence on the roofs.

The provision of museum spaces inevitably implied a total restructuring of these groups of buildings. Indeed, the only original features which have been retained in the project are the façades, the campaniles surmounting the pavilions, and the Duc de Morny State Rooms, along with some of the more outstanding features of palatial architecture, such as the Lefuel and Colbert staircases etc. It was vital to conserve and enhance the high quality palatial features in this part of the Louvre so that – as was already the case with similar features in the cour Carrée and the Denon wing – they could be integrated into the museum cicuits and thus provide continuity in the overall museum sequence.

The rest of the building has been entirely re-arranged. The mezzanines that had been added to the main floors were removed to provide adequate height for the display of works. Furthermore, some of the cross walls were removed to create suitable exhibition spaces. Finally, although the original aspect of the roofs has to a large degree been retained, the roof surfaces themselves have nonetheless been totally converted and provided with indispensible top lighting for the display of paintings. This conversion was a substantial operation, similar to the one carried out at Orsay Museum.

The redeployment of the museum collections around the Napoleon reception area and the Richelieu-Rohan wing led I.M. Pei and Michel Macary to seek appropriate solutions in collaboration with the curators concerned. In the case of the sculptures, where the display setting was closely related to the architecture of the spaces, this was a perfectly logical approach. In other instances, the designers proposed solutions which would ensure maximum flexibility for future museological layouts.

In order to lay down basic principles for the successful functioning of the museum, which will take into account both museological constraints and constraints deriving from the existing building, this type of close collaboration between architects and program designers is vital throughout the entire course of feasibility studies.

### The Richelieu arcade and the internal courtyards

This ground level link has been opened between the place du Palais-Royal and the cour Napoléon. The architecture has been highlighted; in particular, special lighting effects have been provided for the vaulted ceilings.

The lateral openings onto the internal courtyards (the cour du Ministre to the west, and the cour des Caisses to the east) have been enlarged and closed off with large glazed bays which afford new prospects of the courtyards. These courtyards are to be converted into museum spaces for the display of sculptures and this is a fundamental feature of the project. They will be covered by glazed roofs supported on lightweight structures of tubes and cables echoing the web-like appearance of the pyramid structures.

The ground level of the courtyards on either side of the arcade is to be redesigned as a succession of raked tiers that will gradually slope back and meet up on the mezzanine level of the cour Napoléon; in this way, visitors will enter the courtyards from below, and will proceed in stages up to the ground floor of the building. French sculpture will be displayed on the raked tiers.

Ample links will be provided between these spaces and the ground floor level where the window openings are to be enlarged to floor level in order to provide greater transparency and ease visitor flow.

The section of the building between the cour des Caisses and the cour de la Poste will be built in a similar style to the adjacent buildings, and will also feature openings in order to increase transparency between the two courtyards.

Two floors of the building are to be re-arranged

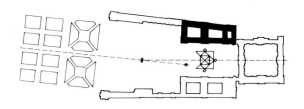

internally and only the façades are to be retained in their original state.

Level 1 corresponds to the level of the terraces overlooking the cour Napoléon. This level contains the Duc de Morny State Rooms, and has been entirely allocated to the Objets d'Art Department.

Level 2 has been reserved for the Paintings Department. The ceilings are to be redesigned to provide natural day lighting from glazed roofs equipped with variable lighting control systems.

Both these floors will be linked to the corresponding floors in the cour Carrée, thus ensuring the continuity of the museum sequences.

A battery of escalators is to be installed in the Colbert wing close to the Richelieu pavilion in order to provide vertical circulation routes between the floors. These escalators will serve the mezzanine level, the Napoleon reception area, the basement, the ground floor, and the second and third floors.

The superb Lefuel staircase located on the rue de Rivoli side has been retained, and has been extended down to the lower level of the cour du Ministre in order to provide continuity to the museum circuits on all floors.

The overall layout is rounded off by elevators which provide access for disabled visitors to all floors.

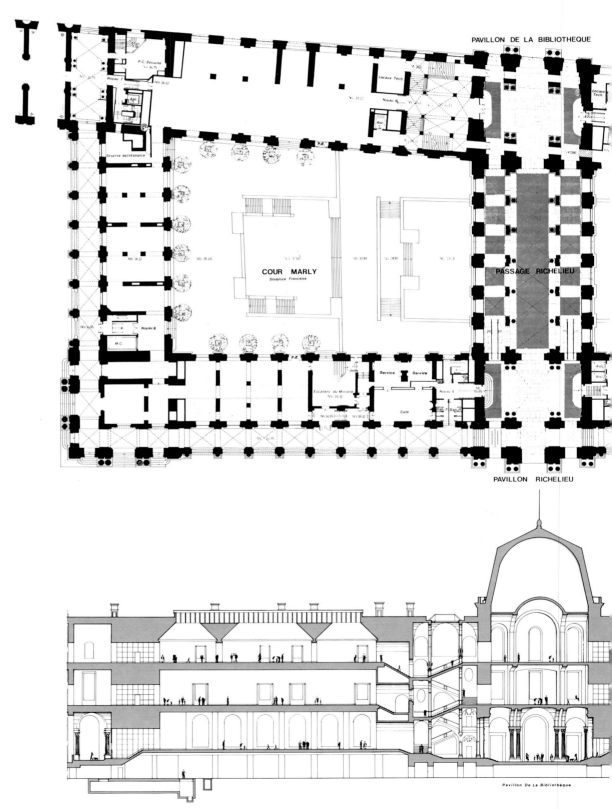

COUR MARLY
Sculpture Française

PASSAGE RICHELIEU

PAVILLON DE LA BIBLIOTHEQUE

PAVILLON RICHELIEU

Pavillon De La Bibliothèque

128

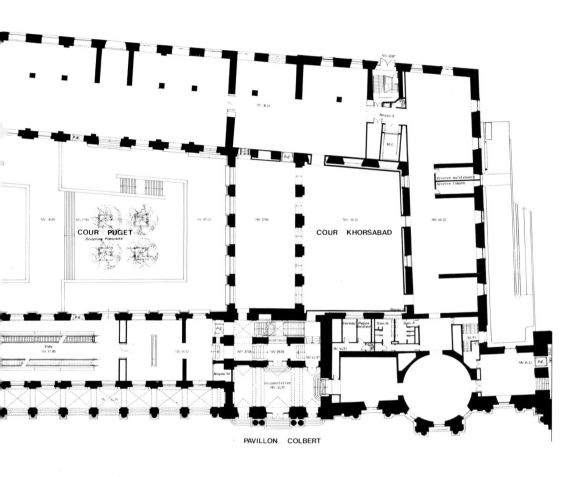

NIV 3987

NIV 36.32

Noyau 3

M.C

Reserve maintenance
Reserve tampon

COUR PUGET
Sculpture Francaise

NIV 3095    NIV 37.93    NIV 35.25    NIV 37.06    COUR KHORSABAD    NIV 36.32    NIV 36.32

P.E

P.E

P.E

Vide
NIV 30.85

NIV 36.32    NIV 37.06    NIV 35.78

Bureau Repos
Gardien    San. H.    San. F.

NIV 34.97    NIV 34.97    34.95

P.E

NIV 36.32

Noyau 1a

Documentation
NIV 34.97

PAVILLON    COLBERT

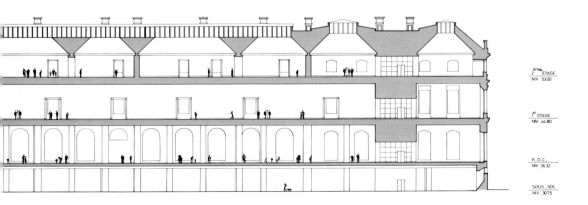

2ème ETAGE
NIV 53.00

1er ETAGE
NIV 44.80

R.D.C.
NIV 36.32

SOUS_SOL
NIV 30.75

## THE PYRAMID

This is the most outstanding feature of the whole scheme – the one which has given rise to the most controversy, and has been subject to the greatest deal of outside pressure. It is, of course, a symbol which expresses the architect's genius.

I.M. Pei wanted the load-bearing structure to be gossamer light, so as to give an unobstructed view of the palace.

From a technical point of view, the result is the outcome of a dialectical process which involved the architect, the engineers and the contractor. As the architect wanted the most transparent and light structure that could possibly be built, the contractor marshalled all his talent to meet such a requirement; meanwhile, he had to ensure the stability of a structure incorporating supporting components which were liable to undergo a foreseeable amount of distortion, and in which variations in dimension would occur as a result of thermal expansion and changing climatic conditions (layers of snow and ice, gusts of wind).

The structure corresponds to the geometrical form defined by the architect, and also meets the constraints of flatness which he stipulated. Protracted calculations and adjustments were necessary to achieve a result which has met with the unanimous approval of everyone concerned – designers, inspectors, and client body.

The pyramid combines two distinct features: the façade, and the supporting metal structure.

### The supporting structures

The glass and steel pyramid rests on steel and concrete structures which are supported by four reinforced concrete posts. The end floor beams have a 38 m span. The architect accepted a thickness of 1.4 m. The slenderness ratio is 1/27; this is high, given the permissible deflection tolerance of 2 cm, or 1/2000 of the overall span. In addition, technical components such as air ducts, cables, lighting appliances, smoke extractor flap mechanisms etc. have been integrated, and the adjacent re-inforced and pre-stressed concrete floors have to bear the considerable load – 5 t/m² – of their own deadload weight plus additional weight.

It was necessary to compensate for the deflection of the end floor girders at each stage of construction, allowing for the gradual increase in load which occurred as the adjacent concrete floors were poured, the pyramid installed in position, and the facing work carried out on the surrounding basins. The metal end floor girders were therefore maintained horizontal by means of tie bars anchored in the ground (pre-flexure).

The tie bars were installed on either side of the supports, and enabled forces equal to the bending loads which would occur at each stage of construction to be applied to the girders; the load could consequently be balanced, and girder defelection kept within the permissible tolerance levels.

Factory counter-deflection was 24 cm, and a tensile stress of 400 t had to be applied via the tie bars in order to remove this.

Thus, throughout the entire construction phase, the vertical deformations of the girders were merely in the order of a few (successively two to four) centimetres, and the secondary effects on the pyramid structures encased in architectonic concrete (in particular, crack formation) were kept under control, while the water basin spillways were maintained horizontal.

The girders were manufactured in the mills of the Strasbourg Foundry Corporation. They were produced in three sections: a main 38 m long section, and two shorter 7.6 m sections which were assembled to the former on site. The main sections – weighing 140 t – were transported from Strasbourg to Paris in a heavy load convoy system comprising two six-axle bogies, a 400HP tractor unit, and a 400HP pusher unit.

## The façade

Once the desired goal (transparency, absolutely plane surfaces) was established, choices had to be made concerning the glazing, the structure and the appropriate assembly procedure.

### The curtain walls

The exterior volume of the pyramid is defined by four inclined plane curtain walls. The glazing is mounted directly on aluminium frames; temporary diagonal struts were used to reinforce these and

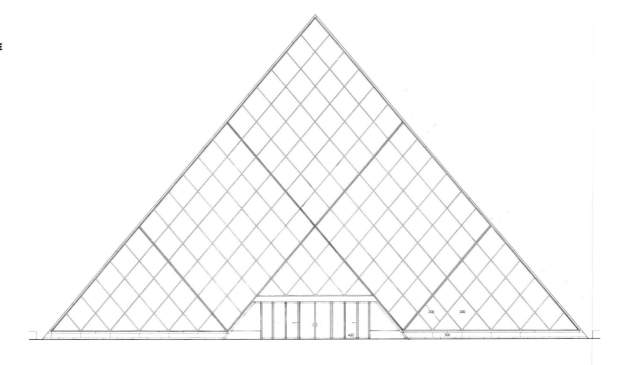

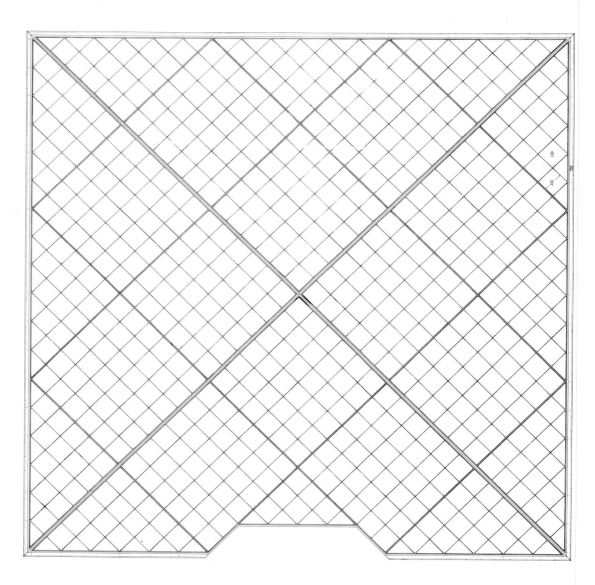

132

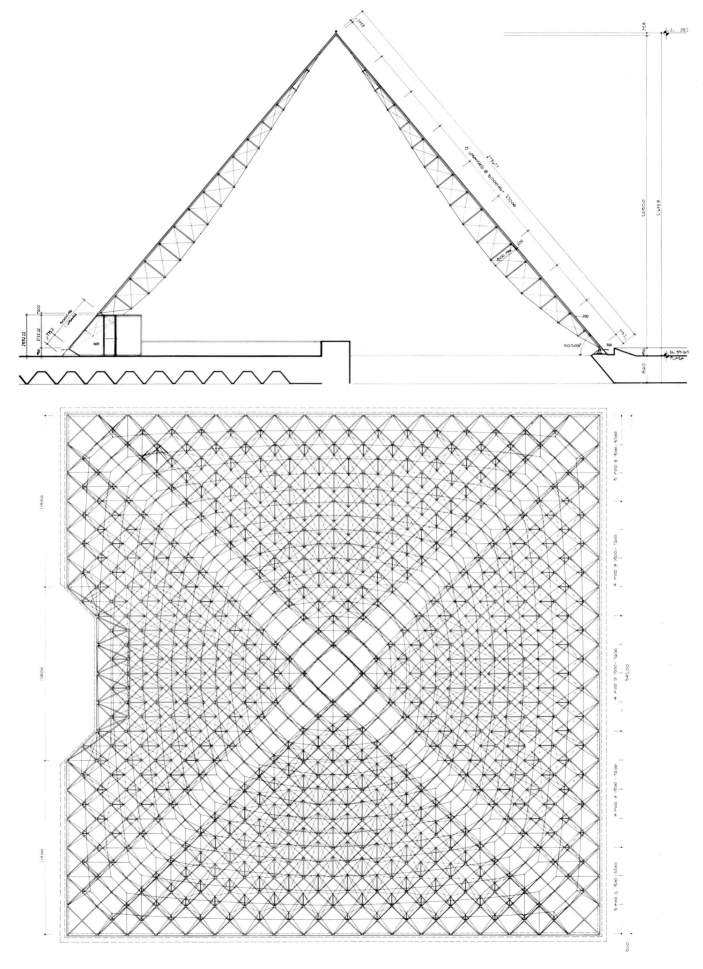

133

to maintain a perfect geometrical shape in the course of construction.

The glazing consists of two 10 mm thick panes of glass which are glued to a 1 mm film of plastic ; this film ensures that the glazing will remain in place should one of the panes break.

### The glass

Choosing the glass was a long and complex process. I.M. Pei wanted a type of glass which would not alter colors. However, owing to the thicknesses in standard use, the high ferrous oxide content in ordinary glass produces conspicuous green tonalities. At the request of the architect, the Saint-Gobain glass manufacturing company conducted an elaborate research program to discover a suitable type of glass. At one point, they were even prepared to irreparably damage one of their normal kilns in pursuit of this objective. Finally, however, it was decided to manufacture the glass in an electric kiln. Although this was a more reliable solution, it excluded the use of modern float system techniques to produce the glass panes. It was necessary to resort an older technique, in which the glass was drawn vertically; this, however, proved an awkward solution, because the panes were no longer flat enough to prevent the visual distortion which the architect had rejected. Accordingly, the panes were sent to the United Kingdom – along with Japan, the only place in the world with facilities where the glass could be polished perfectly plane.

### The structure

The pyramid has a 4 × 34.2 m square base and stands 20.9 m high. Each of the four faces is divided up into diamond-shaped panels, the diagonals of which measure 1.9 m and 3 m. These aluminium panels support the window frames of the glued glass curtain wall. This perfectly flat mesh rests on structures consisting of stainless steel bars and cables which form truss girders perpendicular to the faces of the pyramid.

The compression boom chords run parallel to the load bearing structures of the glazed frames. At each intersection in the mesh pattern – at the top of each of the diamond shapes – a stainless steel bar, perpendicular to the façade, carries the weight of the glazing by means of the thrust from cables that are attached to the lower compression boom chord of the truss and stretch down the base and up to the top of the structures; these cables are rather like the shrouds on a sailing ship that compensate for the strain of the sails on the ship's masts. This reference to the rigging of large sailing ships is not merely theoretical; it is readily apparent in the very details of the assemblages and components used to tighten the cables.

The systematic attempt to minimise the thickness of the structural bars and coupling joints meant that special varieties of steel were used: Z2 CND 17 12 Austen steel and Ugine NSM 21 S for the stainless steel reinforcing bars, and Z6 CND 18

*View of
the cour Napoléon
from the Sully porch.*

12 M (containing 0.05% less carbon) for the moulded couplings. Moreover, both Ugine – the suppliers of the rolled bars – and the Ats-Marlyd and Precimanoir Foundries, supplied components with mechanical properties which were 10% in excess of the maximum performance levels required by current standards.

The compression boom chords and steel bars are welded together onto moulded coupling components. Each of these prefabricated components was designed and made using a traditional technique known as *cire perdue*. This technique alone can guarantee a finish meeting the necessary conditions: that the basic components should leave the foundry precision-made and thus require only minimum machining, and that they should have fine, even facing.

The appearance of the structural features was the object of considerable research.

Thus, the components of the compressed structures – boom chords, bars and couplings – were subjected to several consecutive treatments and all have a mat satin appearance: they were first blasted with stainless steel shot; then they were given a further blasting with glass shot; finally, they were steeped in diluted nitric acid for chemical passivation treatment. It proved a highly delicate task to apply these various processes in correct proportion, as the architect insisted on obtaining an even tone and sheen throughout.

On the other hand, those taut parts of the structure consisting of rods have a smooth, shiny appearance; this was obtained by very fine machining, followed by cleaning and chemical passivation.

### Assembling the structure

The bars, rods and cables all had to be accurately and meticulously manufactured so that they could be assembled together; they also required

## THE PROXIMITY OF THE SEINE
## AND THE GEOHYDROLOGICAL
## PROBLEMS INVOLVED

The level of the water table – normally lying 8 m below ground level – depends on the level of the Seine. When the river is in spate, the water table can rise to 4 m below ground level. Fortunately, the site had a favourable geological configuration[1].

Test borings enabled the following geological description to be drawn up:
. a layer of fill from 0 m down to approximately 4 m;
. a layer of recent alluvial sand from 4 m down to approximately 9.5 m;
. a hard limestone layer from 9.5 m down to approximately 24.5 m;
. a layer of cuisien or sparnatian sand from 24.5 m down to approximately 36 m;
. a layer of clay mixed with impurities from 36 m to 56 m.

The danger of seeping river water arose in the case of the initial bed of recent alluvial sand, and also within the lower limestone bed where water could percolate horizontally between the separate sedimentary layers of which the bed was composed. The underground concrete structures of the river-side expressway, however, formed an efficient dam. Using an injection process, a water-tight screen was accordingly built around the excavated zone to prevent lateral seepage. Furthermore, the maximum depth of the underground structures was restricted to − 14 m. Finally, an extensive drainage system was installed beneath the works to collect and drain away into sewers any water that might eventually seep through the screen or down through the limestone bed and the layer of cuisien sand.

This technique avoided the necessity of constructing very thick rafts capable of withstanding water pressure or of building tanks: the pressure was removed by drainage.

Variations in water-table levels were monitored by means of seepage piezometers installed around the site perimeter and beneath the structures.

Using mathematical computer-simulation techniques that allowed for the relative permeability of the soils, the Brgm Geological and Mining Research Office conducted a special survey of hypothetical variations in water-table level in the event a hundred-year flood ocurring (i.e. the maximum level statistically probable over a hundred-year period). This survey was conducted over an area stretching from the Samaritaine department store to the Concorde and covered the entire site of the project.

1. Mean ground level: 34 m ordnance datum.
Mean water table level: 26 m ordnance datum.
Mean ten-year spate level of the Seine: 31 m ordnance datum.

## SAFETY MEASURES

Extremely stringent safety regulations are enforced in buildings frequented by the general public, and such regulations are even stricter where underground spaces are involved.

In the case of the reception space located beneath the pyramid at a level of − 9 m, this entailed the increased provision of fire and smoke-insulated emergency exit corridors.

Occasionally, however, public safety measures were incompatible with the security of the artworks.

Special remote-control systems were installed to operate doors and to ensure surveillance of emergency exit corridors. These exits emerged at ground level inside the cour Napoléon. Given the general layout of the space, the architect insisted upon strict specifications governing the exact locations as well as the means of covering such exits, taking into account the pattern of paving in the courtyard and the proportions and profiling of the palace façades. Such architectural constraints raised numerous problems concerning the insertion of safety corridors in the basement areas.

The Matra corporation therefore designed special hydraulic-jack-operated steel trapdoors that open automatically in the event of an emergency.

The question of public safety and artwork security involved the installation of numerous monitoring and surveillance devices: smoke detectors, cameras, telephone networks, automatic extinguishers, door and lock controls, remote-controls for ventilation and lighting systems etc., all of which are linked to a central control-room where the relevant data is processed, stored in computer files and printed out in hard copy. This necessitated the installation of miles of cable winding through the technical deck located on the lowest level beneath the cour Napoléon programs.

## THE PYRAMID
## GENERAL SPECIFICATIONS

Height: 20.9 m.
Width at base: 34.2 m.
Weight of the structure: 95 tons.
Number of coupling joints: 2150 (6000 bars).
Thickness of glazing: 21 mm.
Dimension of panes: diamond-shaped,
with 3 m and 1.9 m diagonals.
Number of glazed panes: 673
(603 diamonds, 70 triangles).
Weight of glazing: 105 tons.
Net glazed area: 1900 m².
Base area of the pyramid: 1000 m².

very accurate machining: down to a few tenths of a millimetre for the lengths of the bars, rods and coupling arms, and to within less than half a degree for the angles of the coupling arms.

It was possible to assemble some of the parts in the factory; to ensure the tolerance level in the positioning of the couplings, allowance was made for any distortion due to welding. Other parts were welded on site; a scaffolding was erected, on which the components to be welded were carefully positioned. Each welding was then carefully ground, and concealed by means of a sliding stainless steel ring.

Nevertheless, nineteen consecutive stages were required to assemble the entire structure; at each stage, deflection was systematically inspected, and extremely precise geometric checks were carried out on counter-deflection in the course of assembly; this was done by finely adjusting pre-calculated forces and deflections.

The cables were tightened while final adjustment was carried out to the glazing supports, so as to ensure a perfectly plane surface. To obtain the correct tension, the eventual weight of the glazing was simulated by hanging 140 kg blocks of pig iron from each intersection in the mesh.

Once the last-minute geometric checks had been carried out, the glazing was fitted in position from a boat-scaffold suspended from the jib of a mobile crane; as each glazed panel was fitted in place, the corresponding block of pig-iron was removed to maintain the equilibrium of the forces in the load-bearing system.

### The staircase

The spiral staircase linking the belvedere and the reception area is an architectural feature beneath the pyramid; in fact it is a kind of sculpture. It has a single flight, and a extremely slender stringer. The load-bearing metal structure can be compared to a spring that has been layed on the floor of the reception area and fixed to the belvedere. It is shaped like a ship's propellor and has stone steps; these had to be made as lightweight as possible, and have been reinforced with sheets of steel so as to respect the dimensions which the architect stipulated. The guard rails are treated in ultra clear glass and their curving form follows that of the spiralling helix; they are fixed directly into the stringer with no intermediate uprights; the uniform stainless steel handrails are merely glued to the glass components.

The architect has designed a cylindrical elevator platform in the centre of the newel of the spiral staircase; when raised, this elevator fills the entire newel; when lowered, it fits completely into a well-housing in the floor. Safety problems have been overcome, notably by providing sufficient distance between the elevator guard rails and the staircase to rule out any danger of an accident occuring. When the elevator stops, an ingenious system automatically positions a mobile platform to span the gap between the elevator and the top landing.

*The third floor rooms
in the north wing
of the cour Carrée being
fitted out, Spring 1989.*

## THE MUSEUM PROGRAM

Very shortly after the decision was taken to allocate the north wing of the palace to the museum, it became quite obvious that the premises from which the Ministry of Finance was due to move would not suffice to solve all the problems encountered. Once these structures had been adapted to museological purposes, an extra 30 000 m² would be available; although this would be sufficient to re-organize, extend and modernize the exhibition floor areas, it would not allow for three fundamental requirements to be met:

– since it had been built in various stages over different periods, the Louvre palace had no monumental entrance; moreover, it had been the Tuileries – rather than the Louvre – which had majestically symbolized royal power in the past, and had indeed been the seat of such power. As a result, the layout of the present-day Louvre lacked a certain clarity. Although there were several ways into the palace, there no readily obvious main entrance; this was an awkward spatial constraint for a public place;

– within the palace, there were few spaces where adequate public reception and information facilities might be provided in a rational manner. In particular, the configuration of the palace – a series of long, relatively narrow buildings surrounding courtyards – was ill-adapted to the provision of a bookshop, childrens' reception area, lecture hall etc; the rooms were all inter-connected, and thus also served as circulation routes;

– owing to the lack of specific premises for technical and service infrastructures, such facilities had to be provided either in palatial spaces, or in unsuitable premises; moreover, even such spaces were in short supply. Such functional inadequacy had contributed to the deterioration of the palace (the Lefuel and Visconti courtyards were used as service courts; false ceilings had been built in the Napoleon III stables, which housed a staff restaurant and workshops; the painting reserves were accommodated in the corridor des Poules on the third floor of the cour Carrée, etc.).

It soon became obvious that the courtyard basements would also be required. Moreover, the reserves for the Antiquities Departments, along with technical premises, had already been installed there in the 1970s. Once the Ministry of Finance had moved out, the museum would expand around the cour Napoléon, which could then accommodate the reception area, and thus become the hub of the museum.

However, the constraints imposed by the time schedule (the cour Napoleon was unoccupied, whereas the north wing would not be available until Bercy was completed), and the differing nature of

*The Daru gallery prior to the installation of reception and ticket sales beneath the pyramid. The gallery can henceforth be devoted exclusively to the display of Greco-Roman antiquities.*

the problems raised (on the one hand, a new building; on the other, office spaces that were to be converted into museum rooms) naturally implied a stage-by-stage approach.

### Stage 1: defining functions and allocating spaces

Once the Sodeteg/J. Dourdin team had been selected for the programing, architects and program designers worked throughout the year – on the basis of I.M. Pei's sketch which had been approved by the President of the Republic in May 1983 – to provide form for the content of the space to be excavated under the cour Napoléon. The results of this activity – the worked-up architectural design, and a preliminary program – were discussed at the Arcachon seminar where the broad outlines and principal objectives of the project were hammered out in the course of conflicting debate and penetrating argument; today these outlines and objectives – together with the worked-up programs and schemes – still constitute the basic framework of the Grand Louvre project.

Indeed, despite the inevitable alterations which are inherent in a project of such scope, the general approach proposed at that time has not been fundamentally called into question. It is as follows:

1. The reception and service infrastructures are grouped together under the Cour Napoléon. These underground works are linked to the three main pavilions in the palace – Richelieu pavilion to the north, Sully to the east, and Denon to the south. The objectives are:

– to provide the Louvre with a main, central entrance, and adequate reception facilities;

– to provide the palace with facilities for cultural activities;

– to create the technical conditions necessary for the rational functioning of such a large museum;

– to improve working conditions for the scientific, technical and security staff;

– to clear the palatial spaces already used for such infrastructures (the salle du Manège, the Mollien and Denon galleries, and the Lefuel and Visconti courtyards) by removing obsolete facilities which are hardly compatible with the historic décor.

2. The collections are to be entirely redeployed around the new reception area, in new spaces provided in the north wing, and in the re-arranged and modernized rooms of the present museum. Each enlarged department will acquire new spaces which are adapted to the collections, and are easily accessible from the reception.

3. The Central Museums Administration, the *direction des musées de France* and the *Réunion*

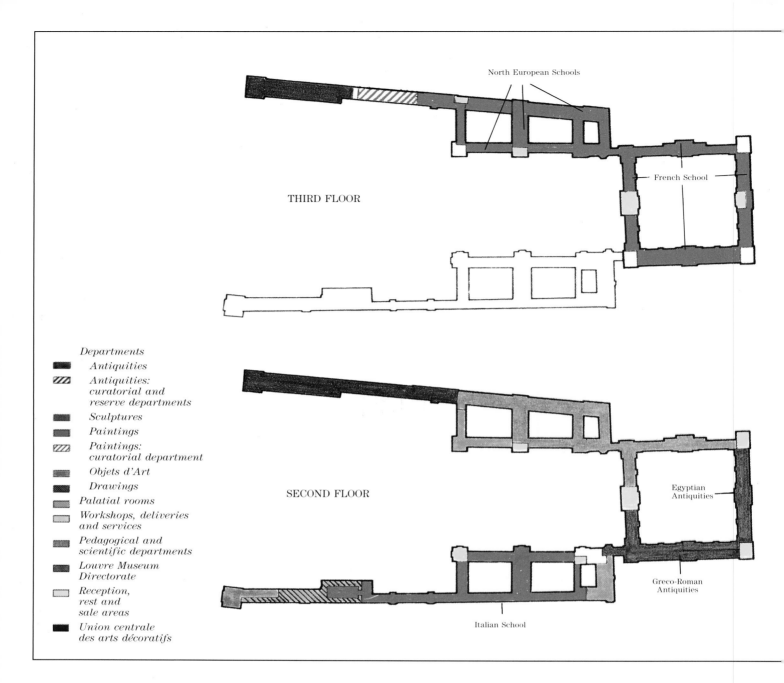

THIRD FLOOR

North European Schools

French School

**Departments**
- ▰ *Antiquities*
- ▨ *Antiquities: curatorial and reserve departments*
- ▰ *Sculptures*
- ▰ *Paintings*
- ▨ *Paintings: curatorial department*
- ▰ *Objets d'Art*
- ▰ *Drawings*
- ▰ *Palatial rooms*
- ▱ *Workshops, deliveries and services*
- ▰ *Pedagogical and scientific departments*
- ▰ *Louvre Museum Directorate*
- ▱ *Reception, rest and sale areas*
- ▰ *Union centrale des arts décoratifs*

SECOND FLOOR

Egyptian Antiquities

Greco-Roman Antiquities

Italian School

*The February 1984 preliminary program. The basic priciples have not changed: the grouping of service and reception infrastructures beneath the cour Napoléon; the redeployment of the collections around this new reception area; the allocation of part of the Flore wing to scientific research and teaching activies.*

Bottom right hand page
*The layout of the collections: the former layout compared with the layout as planned on 1 February 1987.*

*des musées nationaux* are not to vacate the palace straight away. These services will only move in a few years time, allowing the Flore wing and its basements to be allocated to scientific and pedagogical activities (library, laboratory, restoration workshops, the *école du Louvre*) and the Rohan wing to be devoted to scientific and museographic activities (curators' offices and archives, extension to the Louvre and Arts décoratifs collections).

### Stage 2: the working up of the functional and museographic programs

The general approach adopted in 1984 laid the foundations for programming, and involved two distinct rationales:

1. An "organic" program which would determine the main functions to be incorporated in the museum. This included the traditional range of infrastructures required by any modern museum in order to fulfil its role as a cultural, scientific and patrimonial body; such design work was begun

forthwith and resulted in the detailed programs providing a framework within which the architects could proceed.

2. A museographic program which was worked up in two stages:

– the general allocation of the collections within the palace was first defined, in line with the options selected by the curators on the basis of the museum's new morphology, and of the extended floor areas for the collections; it was possible to ensure consistency between the works to be provided in the cour Napoléon and any future museum layout;

– on the other hand, the working up of the detailed programs was not such a pressing matter; for all those responsible, such programs called for further reflection concerning the layout and sequence of visitor routes, and the presentation of the works on display. The Ministry of Finance was not to move out until Bercy was completed; as this move lay several years ahead, it was not deemed

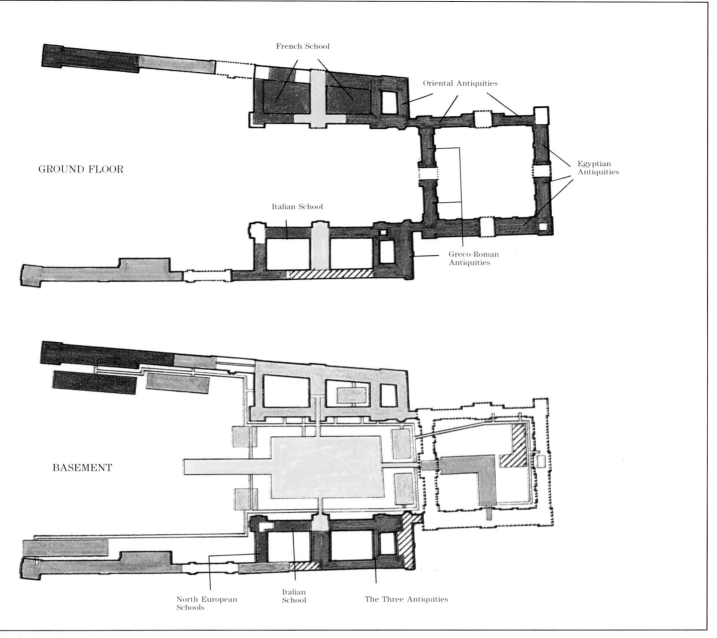

GROUND FLOOR

French School

Oriental Antiquities

Egyptian Antiquities

Italian School

Greco-Roman Antiquities

BASEMENT

North European Schools

Italian School

The Three Antiquities

advisable to finalize the arrangement of the collections down the last detail; indeed, the changing – even ephemeral – nature of exhibition styles, and the subjective aspect involved in the hanging and showing of exhibits could not be disregarded. Moreover, curators and programers were not the only parties involved: the architects and interior designers were also vital participants; they would gradually reveal the constraints and possibilities of the volumes, and thus contribute to displaying the exhibits to best advantage. It was therefore preferable not to proceed too hastily with this phase of the program, and to concentrate all the initial efforts on the facilities to be provided in the cour Napoléon.

## THE ORGANIC PROGRAM

There are certain functions which any museum must necessarily fulfil: security, visitor reception and information, the conservation of artworks etc.

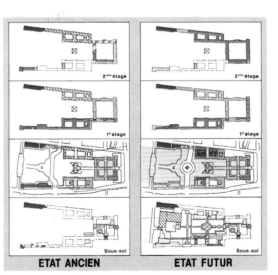

ETAT ANCIEN          ETAT FUTUR

Departments:

of Greco-Roman Antiquities

of Egyptian Antiquities

of Oriental Antiquities

of Sculptures

of Paintings

of objets d'art

of Drawings

Museum Administrative, Scientific and Security Services

Islamic Collections

Union des arts décoratifs

Newly created public open spaces at ground and basement level

143

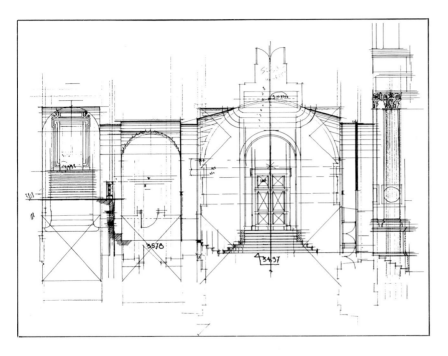

*Sketch
(I.M. Pei and M. Macary)
of the monumental staircases
located in
the Richelieu wing:*
left, *the Colbert staircase;*
right, *the Lefuel staircase.*

and information, the conservation of artworks etc. Fundamentally, the responses which any museum provides in order to meet such requirements differ only in scope: naturally, the number of visitors, and seasonal variations in attendance, have to be taken into consideration, and unwieldy or over-costly facilities are to be avoided.

J. Dourdin and Sodeteg were thus faced with a standard problem of program design; however, the program in question was vast, and the deadlines involved were limited. Moreover, the working up of the initial programs implied a thorough mastery of a constrained and complex spatial framework, as well as familiarity with the museum occupants. It was no simple task for the design team to take stock of all the components of the Louvre; it was an astonishly varied place which was not easily capable of being apprehended at a glance. The initial visits by the team merely enabled them to appreciate the sheer scope of the project ahead.

The variety of buildings and décors, the complexity of a toponymy that was often fully appreciated only by the initiated, and the wealth and diversity of the collections are all factors that combine to make the Louvre a special place. A detour behind the scenes provides one with a glimpse of a veritable "household" with its cubby holes, its make-shift reserve storerooms, its piles of plinths waiting to be restored or used.

Indeed, a similar diversity is to be found among the occupants: curators – sometimes four or five of them together in a windowless room, restorers, research workers, attendants, lecturers, cabinet-makers, monumental masons, tapestry workers

– all of whom have been housed in a haphazard way over the years, as their services have been required.

After a lengthy, painstaking investigation, J. Dourdin's design work resulted in the provision of a straightforward efficient program; this however, did not remove all passion from the debate. At Arcachon, a number of issues came in for particularly fierce discussion.

Among these, was the question of whether the traditional role of the museum should be extended. Ought one to be ambitious in this respect? Ought the Louvre to be turned into something *more* than a museum – a place for cultural experimentation, housing a large public library, accommodation for artists, and facilities for adult education?

To those acquainted with the museum, this seemed a risky – even utopian – course to adopt, because it ignored the realities of the place; as a unique depository of testimonies to a wide range of civilizations, the first challenge facing the Louvre was its capacity to put all its treasures on display – and to display them in an appropriate manner. The verdict was final: there remained so much to accomplish in this latter respect within the Louvre that it would have been dangerous to increase the number of cultural facilities which were quite distinct from its vocation as a museum.

The real challenge consisted in turning the Louvre into a pleasant, properly functioning museum; the cour Napoléon ought therefore to be a gateway to the museum itself, and all activities should be provided in the light of this factor.

It was therefore decided:
– that during museum opening hours, the auditorium would be preferably used for activities related to the museum and, outwith such hours, would not be systematically used for symposia or other non-cultural or non – museographic events;
– to provide large floor areas for temporary exhibitions in the Napoleon reception hall so as to have a place which – although in no way intended to rival the galleries of the Grand Palais – would serve as an introduction to the museum and its collections;
– to stress the essential role of the Napoleon reception space as a place providing information on the collections, and visitor orientation;
– to make it possible to reach each of the opposite wings of the museum without any further ticket check. In the reception, I.M. Pei therefore designed an "open access" mezzanine in order to simplify the visitor routes and to shorten the distances between collections in the museum sequence.

By 1989, the design of the facilities in the cour Napoléon which J.Dourdin had worked up on the basis of such options – and which were now translated into I.M. Pei's architectural scheme – provided the museum with a powerful instrument, capable of handling the major problems. Nevertheless, it would be necessary to await the completion of the interior layout of the palace before the facilities could be used fully.

## 1. The new public reception facilities under the cour Napoléon

The reception and orientation area is located beneath the pyramid. It is a public space onto which open various facilities; each of these occupies one, or two, levels of the four corners of the space. Some facilities are run by the museum, or by the "Louvre" section of the *Réunion des musées nationaux* (National Museums Service) (auditorium, temporary exhibitions, educational activities, bookshop, cloakrooms, ticket offices, information desks etc.); concessions for other facilities have been granted to outside partners (restaurants, shopping arcades and car parks).

The facilities are spread out on two levels. On the ground floor, no museum ticket is required for entry, although this may be subject to separate prices (auditorium, audio-visual rooms, temporary exhibitions, brasserie, bookshop, and pedagogical activities – these two latter facilities being also accessible directly from the museum).

On the mezzanine, an entry ticket is required for access to other facilities designed to make the museum visit more attractive (restaurant, History of the Louvre rooms).

Three of the new facilities in the cour Napoléon are of particular significance in providing the Louvre museum with a new role in the cultural life of Paris:

– the auditorium has film and video equipment (35 mm and 16 mm projectors, video projector, Dolby system), and a central role is thus assigned to the projection and recording of images. Furthermore, the configuration and acoustics of the auditorium have been designed in such a way that it makes an ideal concert hall for chamber music. Finally, it has been provided with simultaneous translation equipment and adjacent 40 and 80-seat lecture rooms for symposia.

– the 1800 m² pedagogical activities department in the Napoleon hall can receive either groups or individual visitors who wish to make a brief tour of the collections. The lecturers have at their disposal five rooms which are linked to the central audio-visual unit, and are equiped with videodisk terminals for presentation and commentary of the visit; the young people's space caters especially for groups of schoolchildren and teachers, and provides an enjoyable introduction for one-day educational visits. A mediathèque, workshops and a refectory are notable features.

– the 1235 m² temporary exhibition space consists of four sections which can be combined into one single section whenever this is required.

Michel Laclotte, the Director of the Louvre Museum, foresees three types of exhibition:

1. Graphic Arts exhibitions, to introduce the general public to the rich collections in the Drawings Department, located in the Flore wing.

2. Recent acquisitions in the Louvre.

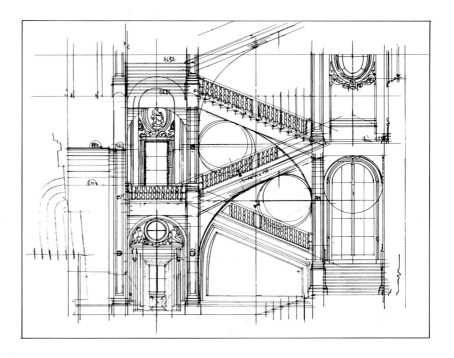

3. Major exhibitions, along with complementary activities organized by the auditorium and cultural departments (symposia, lectures, debates, films produced by the Louvre etc.). Such exhibitions will frequently be interdisciplinary and will be organized along three main lines:

– "History of the Louvre and of the arts in France"; these will evoke landmarks in the history of the arts in France – a history in which the Louvre plays a vital role;

– "Collections in the Louvre"; the idea is to bring together items which are normally on display in different departments, or which are scattered between the Louvre and other museums, in order to highlight such collections in a novel manner;

– "The Ancients and the Moderns"; the aim is to devote a series of exhibitions to the relationship between art of the past and modern art; this is in line with a tradition at the Louvre; the palace was open to living artists from the late 17th century, and regularly exhibited the art of its day up until the mid-19th century (the Salon was held in the salle Carrée, at the eastern end of the Grande Galerie).

Finally, there is an 800 m² exhibition space devoted to the history of the palace and museum. This is located at the entrance to the mediaeval fortified castle, and provides a brief overview of the Louvre, and of the role which it has played in the history of France. The introductory display has been conceived by Pierre Quonian and staged by Richard Peduzzi. It features graphic documents, works of art, and scale models illustrating the main stages in the building of the palace.

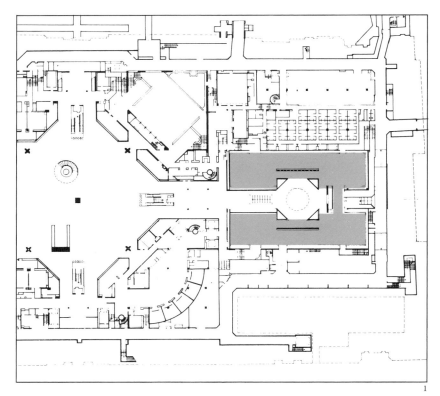

1

3

*The temporary
exhibition rooms created
beneath the cour Napoléon.
Spatial layout and
furnishing designed
by Jean-Michel Wilmotte.*

*1. Location plan.*

*2-6. General views
and details of
three of the modules:
rectangular plinth and
wall-mounted display
window encased
in shot-blasted steel
panelling (4 and 5);
metal guard rail (6).*

*7 and 8: Computer
simulation of
the space and showcases.*

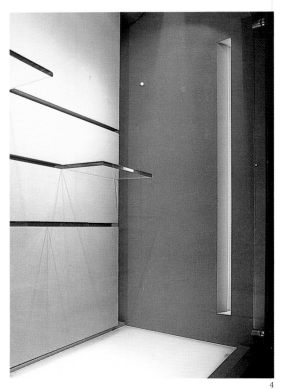

2

4

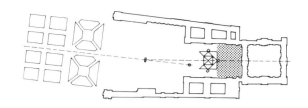

5

6

7

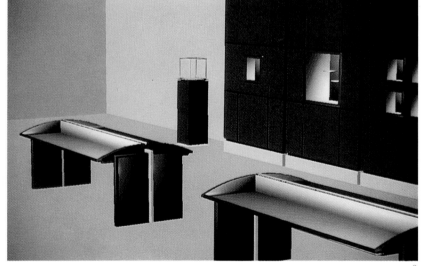

8

## 2. The public reception and information facilities within the museum

Although the Louvre has been made more tight-knit, it is still a vast place which is not easily taken in at a glance. It merits several visits, and lengthy ones at that.

It is impossible, however, to spend half a day in a museum lacking adequate facilities. Although the reception infrastructures provided under the cour Napoléon have vastly improved the situation, they are not sufficient. Facilities for documentation, relaxation, finding one's bearings in relation to the cour Carrée, the Seine, the Carrousel gardens, and the cour Napoléon , must be available to the public throughout the entire visit.

It has therefore been decided:
 – to provide places within the museum where visitors can escape for a moment into the fresh air. A number of areas – often in superb settings – are ideal for this purpose; these include the Lefuel and Visconti courtyards which, for the moment, are used by the museum technical departments, and the terraces on the second floor of the palace, near which café facilities could be provided;
 – to provide specially adapted relaxation areas within the museum; these will feature an information desk – manned by specialist staff – where the visitor can obtain information on the neighbouring collections. A prototype zone is planned in the Sully room once the new layout of the rooms containing the French School has been completed. A pragmatic approach is envisaged – the amount of information available will depend upon the collection, the variety of works on display, and the particular needs involved. Whereas the modern sections – objets d'art, paintings, sculpture – merely require a single general information/documentation room to be provided either at the beginning or the end of the section, fuller information will be necessary in the archaeological sections; in the latter departments, maps, chronological details, and information on the use of various objects on display are often indispensable features. The curators of such departments – faced with a flow of visitors who have litte knowledge of the subjects, and are often young people – wish to provide geographical and cultural background information to the works on display. In view of this new type of public, the Head Curator in the Egyptian Antiquities Department, Jean-Louis de Cenival, is thus inclined to return to Champollion's conception of the museum, *"the concept of a museum as a means of reconstructing an entire civilization in all its aspects (including art), rather than as a place for aesthetic enjoyment or the study of art history; although some people have violently opposed such a view, it remains a seminal approach to the idea of the museum."* [1]. For these archaeological departments,

a series of rooms devoted to the history of civilizations concerned, is to be provided throughout the entire sequence, wherever it is possible.
 – to install visitor information facilities while avoiding a glut of documentation which merely ends up obscuring the works themselves. In this vein, a consistent, integrated visitor direction system is to be provided; a standard system of presentation and signposting is used throughout the entire museum sequence. Visitor directions constitute the minimal "Ariadne's thread" required to guide the public through the rooms and exhibits and to provide information on the way. These directions should be easily identifiable and clear to follow, yet should maintain a low profile in relation to the works on display. The systematic use of audio-visual material in close proximity to the collections was rejected on the grounds that it would merely be noisy and confusing. On the other hand, new technologies may often prove a valuable asset in specific instances: certain works are difficult to appreciate if they are not placed in context. To meet this requirement, design work has been undertaken on a prototype non-audio, interactive videodisk for the display featuring an isolated fragment of the Panathenaics frieze from the Parthenon. Once this has been in use for a few months, and providing the experiment proves successful and adapted to a museum with a visitor flow such as the Louvre, the procedure may be extended to other exhibits.
 – to increase the number of rooms devoted to introductory display units covering each department. These will feature special facilities for the presentation of frequently renewable small-scale displays.

## 3. The "back-stage" scientific and technical departments

These departments are just as vital to the running of the museum as the reception facilities, and have been designed with a view to the specific requirements of the cour Napoléon, and the Flore and Rohan wings.

As regards the reserve storerooms for artworks, capacity for the Greco-Roman Antiquities has been enlarged to 1900 m² under the cour Napoléon, where new 2030 m² painting reserves have also been created. A further 470 m² for objets d'arts, and 900 m² for sculptures are planned under the courtyards in the Richelieu wing.

Museographic workshops – essential for the everyday running of museum displays, emergency repairs, the setting up of exhibitions or the transport of artworks – have acquired new premises on the lower level of the Richelieu wing ; areas for storage and materials have already been provided under the cour Napoléon.

The *musées de France* laboratory – hitherto installed in makeshift premises in the Flore pavilion – is vital to conservation activities. In the program, the laboratory has been provided with an extra 3400 m² area of underground spaces beneath the

---

1. J.-L. de Cenival, *Le Louvre, sept visages d'un musée,* Paris, éditions de la Réunion des musée nationaux, 1986.

cour du Carrousel and these will henceforth accommodate the Aglae elementary particle accelerator, the first particle accelerator in the world to be used for museological purposes.

Some of the National Museums Service restoration workshops are essential in as huge a museum as the Louvre, and these are to be installed near the laboratory in the Flore pavilion.

The library is also located in the Flore wing, near the *école du Louvre* and the Drawings Department, and has reserves under the cour du Carrousel.

The cloakrooms for the security staff and the workshops, the relaxation rooms and union premises, as well as the staff restaurant, have been laid out under the cour Napoléon. Offices for the administration, the curators and related departments, are to be provided in the parts of the palace already laid out for such purposes (Mollien pavilion, the mezzanine floor in the south wing, top floor in the Rohan wing). The offices at present situated in the south wing of the cour Carrée are to be replaced by exhibition rooms.

From the avenue du Général-Lemonnier – which is now an underpass – there is access to more appropriately laid out delivery areas which are under constant security surveillance. These are linked to the *voie de desserte intérieure, Vdi* (Internal Service Route) which runs round the cour Napoléon; this extends to the end of the cour Carrée; and serves all the reserve storerooms. The Internal Service Route is linked to the museum rooms by service elevators (existing elevators which had been modernized, plus newly created ones).

## THE MUSEOGRAPHIC PROGRAM

When the major museographic options were examined in 1983, no particular approach was systematically rejected. Some people dreamed of making a radical change : objets d'art , paintings and sculptures would be displayed together in "period rooms". This approach had been fashionable for a while in American museums, but was out of keeping with the way in which the Louvre collections had been gradually built up, layer by layer – a process which had left an indelible mark on the collections themselves. Others took an opposing point of view, and wished to push the historical dimension of the Louvre collections to extremes, by creating seven separate museums, thus confirming the already traditional division into seven departments: Oriental Antiquities, Egyptian Antiquities, Greek and Roman Antiquities, Graphic Arts, Objets d'Art, Paintings and Sculptures.

The museum authorities eventually opted for a compromise solution which respected realities and history alike, yet which did not exclude innovation. As has been already mentioned, the arrangement adopted for the collections has taken into consideration the specific nature of each of these in a rational manner:

Above
*Room housing the sequence of paintings by Rubens illustrating The life of Queen Marie de Medici. This sequence – at present incomplete – is to be displayed in full in the Richelieu wing on the third floor of the main pavilion.*

Opposite
*The Campana gallery: the display will remain unaltered but the gallery is to be modernized.*

– owing to their weight, sculptures and archaeological bas-reliefs are on the ground floor. This, moreover, enabled works to be exhibited outdoors in covered courtyards; they could thus be exhibited in natural surroundings while being protected from atmospheric pollution;

– paintings are on the top floor so that they can benefit from toplighting wherever possible;

– the objets d'art, ceramics collections, and objects from Antiquity are displayed in the spaces on the second floor of the palace, most of which are lavishly decorated.

In such circumstances, it was difficult to create seven museums, each having a separate entrance from the outside. Nonetheless, links were provided, and innovations introduced each time that the collections and the spaces permitted. Thus, common display rooms for the "Three Antiquities" have been provided in the south wing of the palace, where the *école du Louvre* is at present located, and under the salle du Manège, around the Visconti courtyard: the purpose is to present archaeological ensembles, and series of works of the Late Antiquity

149

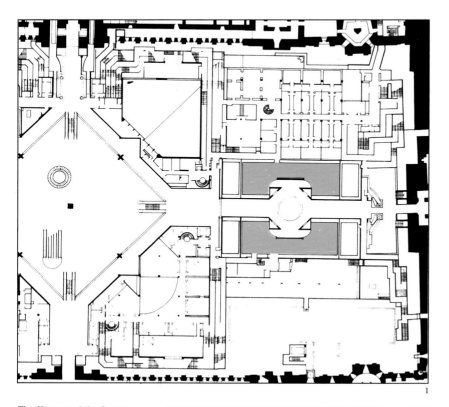

*The History of the Louvre exhibition rooms created beneath the cour Napoléon. Spatial layout and furnishing designed by Richard Peduzzi.*

*1. Location plan.*

*2 and 3. Design model.*

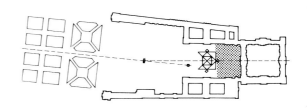

Opposite, and
left hand page right
*The completed space before*
*works and models*
*are placed on display.*
*The display screens*
*are in Oregon pine.*
*The glazed ceiling creates*
*a sky-like effect;*
*the floor has been treated*
*in grey pietra serena paving;*
*the edges of the screens*
*have been given*
*an amalyte treatment*
*that brings depth*
*and lightness*
*to the labyrinthine space.*

RICHELIEU

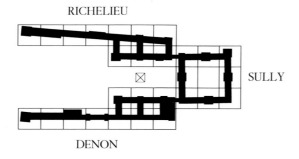

SULLY

DENON

RICHELIEU

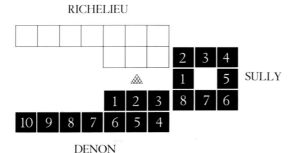

SULLY

DENON

period from the Mediterranean basin (portraits from Fayoum, lead sarcophagi from the Lebanon, sculptures of the cult of Mithra, the Baouït monastery, etc.) At present, depending upon when they were discovered and cataloged, these collections are dispersed between the three Oriental, Egyptian and Greco-Roman Departments; bringing them together will allow the complex Mediterranean civilization of the period to be fully reconstituted.

For similar reasons, a policy has been favoured of bringing Italian paintings and sculpture, Mediaeval or Renaissance sculptures and objets d'art, closer together spatially; although, in a place as vast as the Louvre, this has not done away with the inevitable coming and going involved in following the museum routes in a logical sequence, it has considerably reduced the distances separating these different collections.

The allocation adopted in 1984 also takes into consideration the existing rooms and their history. If the museum sequence were entirely altered, then the Louvre might no longer be the Louvre. It is impossible to dissociate the Charles X museum from the antiquities on display there; or the Campana gallery from its Greek vases; or the Red Rooms in the Mollien wing from the large 19th century French paintings (David, Delacroix, Géricault etc.).

On the other hand, however, were the Louvre to be piously conserved in its historical state, there was the danger that it might remain over – complicated and unfathomable for all those unfamiliar with the place. In some instances therefore, rational presentation of the works had to prevail over the

desire to conserve intact the renowned process of accretion that had been the hallmark of the museum collections. Out of consideration for a public confronted with such a profusion of works on display, it was necessary to simplify visitor circuits; at times, this entailed re-arranging the former museum layout and meant that difficult choices often had to be made.

A "master-piece circuit" was even mooted as part of such plans for re-organization, but this idea was swiftly rejected by the curators. They felt that it was a facile solution, and furthermore, one that represented a patronizing attitude towards the museum visitors. The museum ought to remain a place of discovery and curiosity; if the outstanding works were grouped together then the visitors would have fewer opportunities to personally discover a fascinating work by chance in the course of their visit. After all, the sheer profusion of works on display is surely a central feature of the Louvre.

Such reflections were all incorporated into the overall proposal for the re-allocation of works that was drawn up on the basis of the curatorial programs described below.

From the Napoléon reception hall, visitors have three entrances to the different museum circuits:

*1. To the south (Denon entrance)*
– copies of antiquities: these are either Renaissance works based on Greco-Roman sculptures, or copies belonging to the Borghese and Albani collections. Hitherto dispersed in the Greco-Roman Antiquities and Sculpture collections, they are now on display in the salle de Manège;
– Greek and Roman antiquities: the department has retained its present rooms – which have been recently re-arranged – and has been extended to the second floor in the west part of the south wing of the cour Carrée, as well as under the Daru gallery;
– Italian sculptures: these are housed on the upper and lower ground floors of the Mollien Gallery around the Lefuel courtyard; they are thus more centrally located than in the Flore wing ;
– Italian paintings: these are hung in the Grande Galerie and in adjacent rooms.

*2. To the east (Sully entrance)*
– the History of the Louvre and the mediaeval moats;
– Egyptian antiquities: these have retained their present rooms and have been extended to the second floor in the south wing of the cour Carrée;
– objets d'art, Greco-Roman antiquities and French paintings: these may be reached via the Sully pavilion (Henri II and Henri IV staircases) although this is not the main entrance to the collections.

*3. To the south (Richelieu entrance)*
– Oriental antiquities: these have been re-arranged around the cour de la Poste, and in the

**THE VISITOR DIRECTIONS SYSTEM**

The general approach conceived by the Carbone-Smolan Agency and executed by ADSA is based on a system of precise localizations (addresses) that do away with the necessity of altering signposting each time that collections are moved; this will be a major advantage in the years to come when there are drastic changes in the layout of the collections.

The key features of the system are as follows:
– the museum is divided into three geographical zones – Denon, Sully and, later, Richelieu – with three corresponding entrances from the Napoléon reception area (see top left hand page). The collections on display in each zone are described on the information panels located under the pyramid belvedere;
– each zone is sub-divided into numbered areas (see top left hand page);
– each floor of the museum has been allocated a specific color (see above);
– color-coded signposts have been provided that allow visitors to locate the zone, area and floor (see above);
– each visitor is given a regularly-updated brochure listing the current locations of the collections and principal masterworks (opposite).

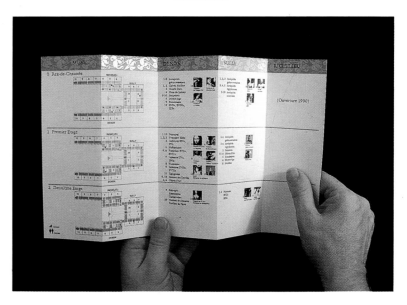

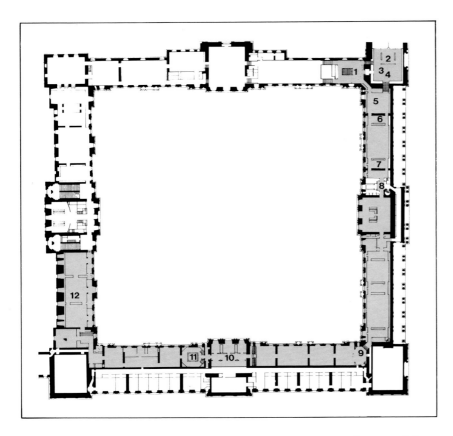

*Plan of the third floor on the Cour Carrée. The grey shading shows the rooms that are to accommodate the French Painting collections – competition winning design by Italo Rota.*

## Renovation of the display conditions and of the approach of the collections

The Louvre museum originally emerged from the encyclopaedic tradition: the accumulation of artworks is such that it sometimes seems to lack any coherent design; the desire to "display everything" is often at odds with the aim of "displaying appropriately". The Grand Louvre project henceforth allows smaller-scale displays to be envisaged – something hitherto inconceivable – in which the unique qualities of the works can be better highlighted.

The increased display areas have not meant that methods of display inherited from the past have been systematically rejected. It must be repeated that such methods are often perfectly tuned to the lavish wealth of the Louvre collections, and that they constitute a precious testimony to museographic tradition. On the other hand, the curators now have at their disposal spaces which permit new types of display.

The fact that the display areas have been doubled does not mean that twice as many works are to be exhibited. Despite the tenacious myth, according to which the cellars of the Louvre are brimming with treasures, most of the works which are cataloged and which merit display are in fact on show – either in the Louvre, or in provincial museums which are beneficiaries of such reserves. There are, however, three exceptions: the very large works, for which there is no suitable room in the Louvre at present (paintings by Coypel and Jouvenet, battle scenes by Le Brun, the Qabr Hiram mosaics, the Scipio historical tapestries); series of works such as the Roman painted stucco portraits kept in the Egyptian Antiquities reserves; and the Islamic collections which also require a larger room than the present day department has at its disposal. Naturally, the Grand Louvre will include rooms for such works, unless their sheer size rules this out, as in the case of the 19th century Néoramas which require 17 m high display screens!

Finally, there are the works which cannot be shown in their present condition, and which require lengthy and costly restoration before they can be exhibited; strenuous efforts are being undertaken to prepare such works for public display.

If any treasures *do* exist in the reserves, they consist in the thousands of objects which are liable to be of interest to the researcher and the connoisseur alone. These include objects in the archaeological departments which have been brought back from digs, and which are far from being all suitable for display – they are a sealed book to all but the expert. From the 19th century onward, the Oriental, Greek and Roman, and Egyptian collections were indeed built up in part as a result of the excavations carried out around the Mediterranean basin. In this way, the French archaeological tradition endowed the national collections with major works such as the Olympia marbles, the frieze of

north wing and west half-wing on the ground floor of the cour Carrée;

– French sculptures: these are housed in the cour du Ministre and the cour des Caisses, and in the adjacent buildings;

– Islamic collections: in the south wing basement in the Richelieu wing;

– objets d'art: these have been extended to the second floor of the Richelieu wing, as far as the Second Empire State rooms, and to the second floor of the north wing and west half-wing in the cour Carrée;

– paintings of the North European Schools: these are installed on the third floor of the Richelieu wing with the French paintings, which start in the east part of this wing and extend right round the cour Carrée;

– the Drawings Department has been retained in the Flore pavilion and wing, and has been provided with new exhibition spaces where the Small Paintings Departments are at present located.

However, as well as increasing the available foor area for displays, and reorganizing museum routes, the display and conservation conditions have also been entirely renovated.

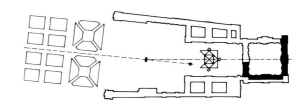

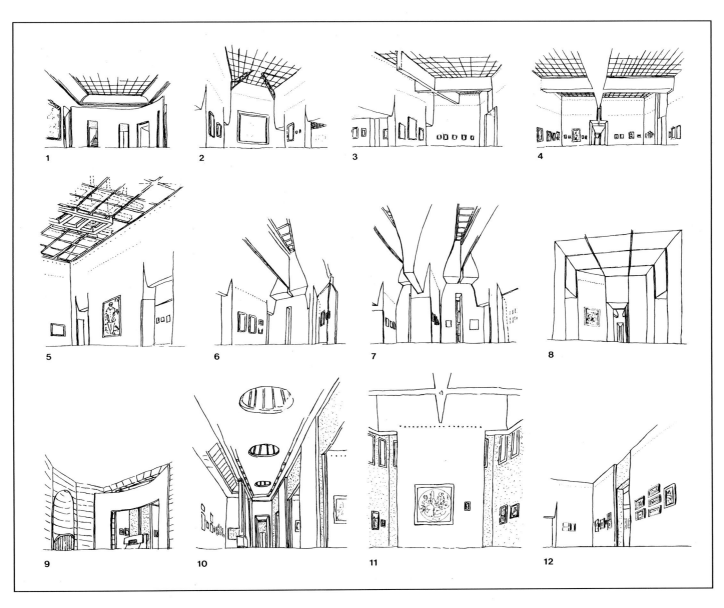

the temple of Artemis from Magnesia, the glazed brick panel of the Archers of the Guard from the palace of Darius, the Squatting Scribe, and the vestiges of the Coptic monastery at Baouit. The research work involved in such major excavations justified the cataloging, analysis and conservation of thousands of fragments; these are of vital importance to research workers, but of little interest to the layman.

Such works and objects – which contribute to the museum's role as a locus for scientific research – will be made more accessible in the Grand Louvre project in two ways:

*Italo Rota's competition proposal for the sequence of rooms (the numbers also refer to the plan on the left hand page).*

*1. The start of the sequence looking towards the Louis XIV room.*

*2, 3 and 4. The Louis XIV room.*

*5. The Watteau room.*

*6. The Watteau room: smaller paintings.*

*7. The Chardin room.*

*8. View towards the Restout room.*

*9. Corner room between the east and south wings with sales desk.*

*10. Small sketches and drawings room in the pavilion des arts.*

*11. The Ingres room.*

*12. The Thomy-Thierry room.*

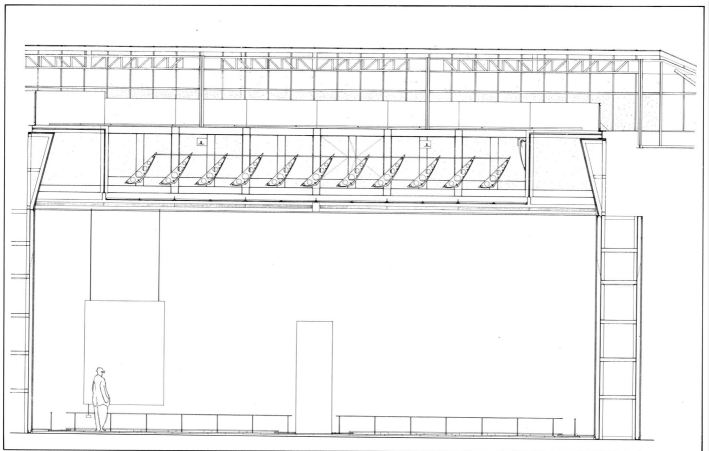

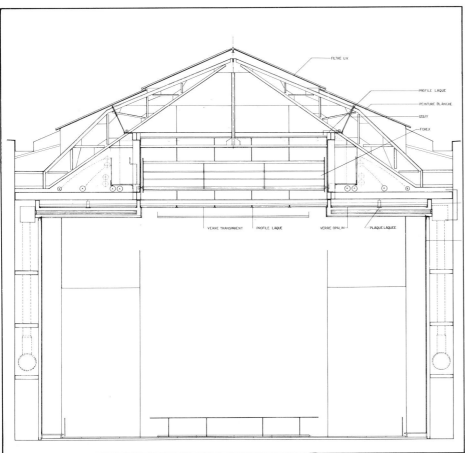

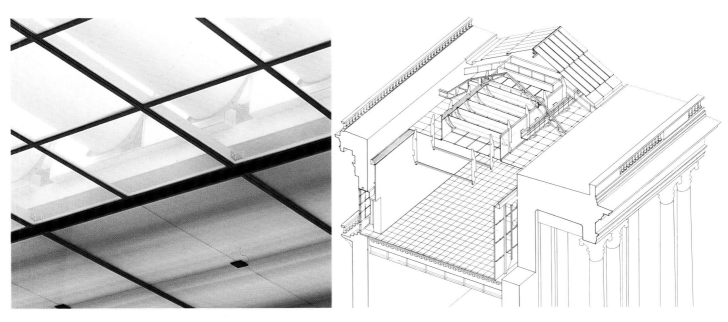

*The toplighting system designed by Italo Rota in the east wing of the cour Carrée for the French painting collection:*
*photos of the design prototype;*
*longitudinal section (left hand page);*
*cross section (opposite).*
*Top, axonometric section of the roof.*
*Adjustable slanting metal plates housed between the glazed roof and the flat transluscent panes of the false ceiling permit natural lighting intensity to be varied according to weather conditions and season.*

– by the creation of modern reserves under the various courtyards. These are veritable work spaces where the curators can catalog, class, photograph and analyse their collections, and which will be open to researchers;

– by the laying out of research galleries which, although open to the general public, will first and foremost cater for researchers and connoisseurs.

Ease of access to the works, and new methods of display consitute the primary requirements of the Grand Louvre.

However, the project ought furthermore to seek to improve the conditions of conservation and protection of the works. Unfortunately, the sheer number of visitors is a factor which is at loggerheads with the patrimonial vocation of the museum. It is therefore vital to provide air-conditioning in most of the rooms containing paintings and wooden objets d'art and sculptures, and, for obvious security and conservation reasons, to protect more of the works in showcases – this will prove time-consuming, but is a vital operation.

Much thought has already gone into the collections which are to be displayed in the Richelieu wing, and on the third floor of the east, south and west wings in the cour Carrée. In constant collaboration with the architects – who are familiar with the building and who are exploring its possibilities and tackling its constraints – the curators are in the process of working up the display programs; they are gradually outlining the form which tomorrow's Louvre shall take.

### The installation of the French paintings on the third floor of the cour Carrée

Within the framework of the Museums Program Law, a major museographic project – involving the installation of French paintings on the third floor of the cour Carrée – had already been planned for the existing Louvre. Naturally, with the programming of the Grand Louvre, this project was confirmed, and is well underway, since the rooms in the west half-wing and the north wing are to open to the public at the same time as the cour Napoléon. The layout of these rooms has been designed by Joseph Motte, and they will offer the public a totally renovated presentation of the French School, from the primitives to the 17th century.

As most of the spaces leading on from these rooms were available (they housed a few offices and workshops, and some impracticable reserves which have been replaced by the new premises created under the cour Napoléon) it was decided, quite logically, to straightaway pursue the new layout within the framework of the Grand Louvre project. A competition was organized, and the commission was awarded to Italo Rota.

The architect used the configuration of the existing building – with its galleries and pavilions – to add variety to the museum sequence and to break up its linear monotony. The approach adopted as regards lighting is based on the use of natural

lighting: a system of operable shutters installed above the transparent glazed roofs enables a relatively constant degree of luminosity to be maintained throughout the day at all seasons, while visitors have an uninterrupted view of the sky and the light outside.

Describing his conception of the display, Italo Rota sees the Louvre as *"an accretion of different collections, a collection of different museums, a spatio-temporal accumulation of museographic conceptions... The sequence of "masterpieces" – which are important for a variety of reasons (artistic, historical or social) – provide the basic features in the conception of the collection, and thus create its image; around these, the other works are arranged in ways which invite corresponding regards and enquiries, and this, in turn, enhances the overall evocation."* [2].

### The redeployment of the collections in the Richelieu wing

Rather than resulting in the juxtaposition of two separate places – the present museum in its old, palatial accommodation, and a new museum housed in a building strictly redesigned for this purpose

2. Extract from the memorandum submitted by Italo Rota in the competition organized by the *établissement public du Grand Louvre* in 1985.

– the simultaneous modernization and extension of the collection spaces should carry over the spirit of the Louvre into the Richelieu wing: such is the challenging aim facing the architects.

*The building*
The group of buildings occupied by the Ministry of Finance – although designed from the very outset for use as administrative premises – has fortunately retained much of the atmosphere of the palace and its history. This wing notably houses the Duc de Morny's State Rooms which have remained intact – even down to their original function. It also boasts architectural features such as the Lefuel staircase, and the Colbert staircase, two of the most monumental staircases in the Louvre. It is essential that such features be highlighted, in order to create a closer link with the existing museum. In a similar vein, the configuration of the north wing, which is made up of groups of long buildings surrounding courtyards punctuated by the pavilions, will allow a characteristic feature of the Louvre – alternating galleries and high ceilinged rooms – to be re-created.

Although the palace has not been swallowed up by the museum, it nonetheless has to comply with constraints implied by the latter: the display conditions (lighting, humidity, security), the logical sequences of exhibits, and the impressive size of certain works, are all criteria which govern the architecture, yet do not indefinitely freeze the museum in a set mould; a relative flexibility is necessary if the curators of tomorrow are not to be shackled by the museography of today.

As in any museum, new acquisitions, donations, and works on temporary loan, make the mobility of the exhibits – with the exception of monumental items – an intrinsic feature.

*The collections*
Apart from the entire French sculpture collection, the Richelieu wing shall house:
– the Mesopotamian collections: the code of King Hammurabi, and the statues of Gudea – the first testimonies to Sumerian civilization, vestiges of the palace of Khorsabad, etc.;
– the collections of objets d'art from the Middle Ages to the 16th century, and from the 19th century, in the extension to the Second Empire salons;
– the French Primitives and paintings from the North European School (Flanders, Holland, Germany, England) – one of the major painting collections in the Louvre.
The scenographic design was worked up at the stage of the detailed preliminary scheme; however, since 1984, M. Macary had carried out a more thorough examination of particularly problematic cases:
– the presentation of the Marly sculptures in the cour du Ministre, and of Puget's sculptures in the cour des Caisses;
– the presentation of the great decorative reliefs from the Khorsabad temple in the cour de la Poste; a more appropriate museographical treatment of the original setting of these vestiges is to be provided;
– the provision of a new room for the sequence of paintings by Rubens illustrating The Life of Queen Marie de Medici, on the top floor of the Richelieu arcade;
– the creation of tapestry galleries on the second floor for the Maximilian's Hunts sequence, and the Scipio tapestries, only some of which are at present on display;
– the reconstitution of the original wood panellings from the King's State Chamber.

*The Scheme*
The worked-up design scheme submitted by I.M. Pei and M. Macary provided a gradual response to these overall requirements. Once the constraints in scheduling that had arisen from the earlier plan to vacate the Finance Ministry stage-by-stage had been removed, it was possible to resume design work on a new basis. At the present stage (the preliminary scheme), the main features pertaining to the various factors involved (historic building, museology, architecture, technical aspects) have already been integrated.

The work carried out on the structures has tended to reduce the presence of load-bearing walls and this allows a relative flexibility for eventual layouts.

In order to bring greater unity to the palace, the intersections between the Richelieu wing and the cour Carrée, and between the Khorsabad courtyard and the Colbert building, have been designed on similar lines to the corresponding spaces located south of the cour Napoléon.

After lengthy discussions concerning the overall museum sequence, visitor circuits have been defined and these now include new escalator access from the cour Napoléon to the various floors in the Richelieu wing.

Finally, a survey of natural lighting in the paintings rooms was carried out with a view to reconciling the contradictory requirements of enhanced display conditions on the one hand, and conservation problems on the other. The amount of light has to be reduced without adversely affecting the presentation of the works; the top-lighting from the ceiling above ought to fall on the display screens where the works are hung, and not on the floor. Although matters are still at a theoretical stage, eventual solutions have been already envisaged.

A process of rethinking the Louvre is underway and this process shall be pursued for many years to come.

For, over and above the places that have been altered and the schemes have already been implemented, much work remains to be done: the seven years anticipated for the project will not be too long a period in which to achieve this difficult balance between modernizing the Louvre while respecting its intrinsic identity.

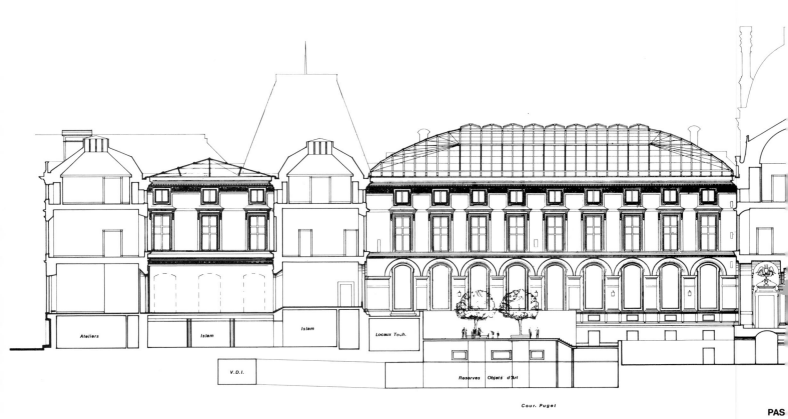

Ateliers    Islam    Islam    Locaux Tech.

V.D.I.    Reserves  Objets  d'Art

Cour. Puget

**PAS**

160

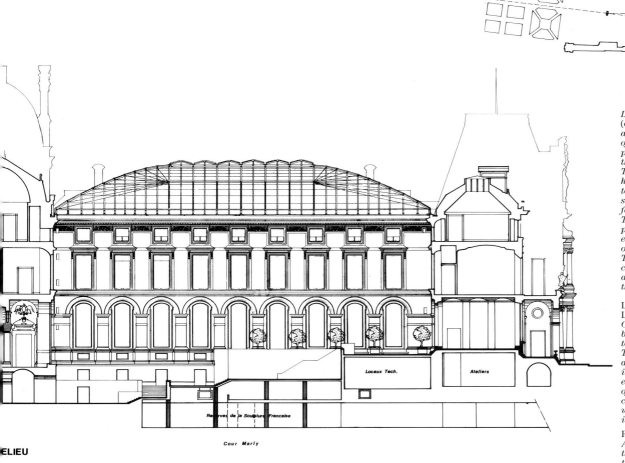

Reserves de la Sculpture Francaise

Locaux Tech.     Ateliers

Cour Marly

Longitudinal section
(opposite)
and cross section (below)
of the I.M. Pei/M.Macary
project for
the Richelieu wing.
The entresol floors
have been removed
to provide
sufficient ceiling height
for the display of works.
Toplighting has been
provided for the painting
exhibition rooms
on the uppermost level.
The three internal
courtyards are covered
and are used for
the display of sculptures.

Left hand page
Left
One of the four Marly horses
being transported
to the Louvre in 1984.
The original statues
are to be displayed
in a pollution-free
environment in the largest
of the Richelieu wing
courtyards while copies
will stand in the old site
in the place de la Concorde.

Right
A winged bull from
the palace of Khorsabad;
the entire sequence
of Assyrian reliefs
is to be dispayed
in the east courtyard
of the Richelieu wing.

Cour Napoléon

Locaux Tech.
Bureau
Locaux Tech.
Bureau
Locaux Tech.
Noyau 2
Bureau
Islam     Locaux Tech.

Cour Khorsabad

Islam

Tapisseries
des chasses de Maximilien

Antiquités Orientales

Locaux Tech.     Ateliers

Rue De Rivoli

Today, at the beginning of 1989, a major phase in the Grand Louvre project is completed. The mediaeval moats and the reception facilities created under the pyramid are to open to the public and the date has been fixed by which the entire departmental services of the Ministry of Economic Affairs and Finance are to move to new premises.

The new place Napoléon has already become a familiar Paris landmark visited by a large and admiring public who enter the square via the Richelieu arcade. The first phase of works constitutes the definitive nucleus of the new Louvre museum – a museum that has opened out to the city and now possesses the reception and service facilities that were sorely lacking in the past.

The museum collections themselves shall be the essential focus of the next phase. The time schedule is crucial and in order to meet the deadlines works shall have to begin in the summer of 1989.

By August 1993, the new layout of the Richelieu wing for museum purposes – the volume is equivalent to that of Orsay museum – and the re-arrangement of the existing museum rooms ought to be largely completed; the bicentenary of the founding of the Louvre museum can thus be celebrated in enlarged and modernized premises that will by then occupy the larger part of the palace buildings. This event will mark the consecration of a two-hundred-year old venture and will highlight the pivotal role played by museums today.

To the west, on completion of the vital parking facilities, the former layout of the Carrousel gardens will have been restored and an uninterrupted pedestrian promenade shall stretch as far as the place de la Concorde.

The unsightly temporary scaffolding has been dismantled to reveal a largely restored palace and façades.

Although further major works are scheduled for 1994 and 1995 – particularly in the Flore and Marsan wings – by 1993, the Louvre museum will have taken on its new definitive form as a public amenity and shall at last possess reception facilities to match the wealth of the collections on display.

In just over ten years, the decision taken by the President of the Republic will have come to fruition, and the Louvre will have been endowed with means and capacities worthy of its reputation as one of the world's greatest museums.

**APPENDIX**
**PROJECT EXECUTION**
**THE OVERALL ORGANIZATION**
**OF DESIGN AND WORKS**

## 1. THE CLIENT BODY

The *établissement public du Grand Louvre* – with outside assistance from a number of technical design offices – constituted the client body.

The Louvre museum curators and the heads of the *Direction des musées de France* and the *Réunion des musées nationaux* (National Museums Service) were directly involved in laying down the fundamental guidelines for the programming, and in ensuring that the projects complied with the programs thus defined.

Pierre QUONIAM, Inspector-General in the *musées de France* Executive and former Director of the Louvre, co-ordinated and steered the joint collaboration between the *établissement public du Grand Louvre* and the future users of the new museum.

The *Direction du patrimoine* Department of the Ministry of Cultural Affairs was associated with the projects for restoration works to the palace, these projects subsequently coming under the supervision of the *Monuments historiques* Inspectorate. The projects were prepared and submitted by the Head Palace Architect, Georges DUVAL, himself an Inspector-General with the *Monuments historiques.*

Finally, archaeological questions came under the supervision of a specially-created historical and archaeological commission chaired by Georges DUBY. This commission carefully monitored all the excavation works carried out in the cour Carrée, the cour Napoléon and the Carrousel gardens.

Jérôme DOURDIN and SODETEG were in charge of museum programming.

The concession for the restaurants and cafeterias located under the pyramid was awarded to the ACCOR corporation.

Five specialized departments under the responsibility of the client body supervised the execution of works in the first phase:
– the Design department supervised, directed and co-ordinated the entire design and programming process;
– the Contracts department monitored the public tendering procedure and liaised with supervisory bodies (the Negotiated Contracts commission, the Grand Louvre public contract commission, and the Central State Commission on public contracts);
– the New Works department was responsible for the supervision of all works other than those relating to the existing palace buildings (contract management, administrative procedures in liaison with the contracts office, time and costs control, settlement of bills);
– the Restoration Works department was in charge of similar tasks for works carried out to the existing palace fabric;
– contract accounting and payments were handled by the Financial department under the general secretary.

The Director had overall responsibility for costs control and subsequent supervision was carried out in turn by the Design department and the works managers.

Among all those who contributed to the success of the project, special mention should be made of Maurice FOISSAC who died in a road accident on 14 August 1987. He had been in charge of the cour Napoléon site under I.M. Pei, a task in which he applied his innate qualities of leadership and efficiency to full adavantage. His memory will always be cherished by those who participated in the project and who now regret his tragic disappearance.

As the *établissement public* operated on a limited staff basis, wide use was made of outside consultants in order to complement the internal organizational structure.

## For design work

A general steering unit, SETEC ORGANISATION – some of whose staff members were delegated to the various teams in the Design department – was given overall planning and supervisory responsibilities in early 1984.
- ADSA (visitor directions)
- AEROPORTS DE PARIS (operational logistics problems and specific problems relating to security, restaurant facilities and visitor flow, etc.)
- AGENCE GROUPE 7 (communication)
- ATGT (survey plans of the Denon and Richelieu wings)
- ATN-CONSEIL (preview of functioning)
- BRGM (geohydrological problems)
- CABINET DELPORTE, LAIGNEAU et AUMOND (consultants for construction cost-estimate analysis)
- CARBONE-SMOLAN (visitor directions)
- LEGRAND-MARTY (survey plans)
- OTH (consultants to the *établissement public du Grand Louvre* for centralized maintenance and optimum-efficency energy management)
- RATP (specialist consultants with experience of below-grade works)
- SAGATEL (telephone systems)
- SEMAH (specialist consultants with experience of below-grade works in a similar site to that of the Louvre)
- SEMA-METRA (main computer networking)
- SETEN (audiovisual technical backup)
- SOFRETU (RATP subsidiary – automatic ticket facilities)

In addition, a number of outside architects were called upon to provide independent supervision of design work.

## For building works

- VERITAS and SOCOTEC (supervision of structures and site safety)
- COPIBAT (organisation, steering and supervision of works in the cour Carrée and the museum of Fashion)
- PLANITEC (organisation, steering and supervision of works in the cour Napoléon and the Richelieu wing)
- BRGM (supervision of existing fabric)

This organisational arrangement adopted by the *établissement public du Grande Louvre* arose from the decision taken to deal separately with each of the groups of related works contracts and from the need for overall supervision of architectural and design work; such an approach was deemed preferable to the alternative solution whereby the architectural and design team would have assumed responsibility for such tasks.

## 2. THE ARCHITECTS AND DESIGNERS

Architectural and design work was carried out by teams of architects and technical design offices in the case of the new works, and, in the case of the restoration works to the palace fabric, by the Head Palace Architect in compliance with the statutory regulations governing works in historic buildings.
New design work was largely the responsibility of I.M. PEI and his team, in collaboration with Michel MACARY and Georges DUVAL, Head Palace Architect, and with the assistance of the SOGELERG and SERETE technical design offices, selected as a result of a competition for the definitive sketch.
Other design teams were allocated ancillary programs:
– Georges DUVAL and OTH, for the laboratory and the delivery zone;
– SEMAH, for the Lemonnier underpass infrastructures, assisted by Georges DUVAL for the architectural treatment to the immediate surrounding area.
The decision that had been adopted to parcel out works in separate tenders, and the high degree of integration between the numerous works and civil engineering contractors, meant that co-ordination between the various tenders and major works on the fabric was necessary. Owing to their intimate acquaintance with the project as a whole, the technical design teams were entrusted with this delicate task under the overall responsibility of the architects.
Moreover, two designers were called in for the interior layouts in the reception programs:
– Jean-Michel WILMOTTE was commissioned with the design of the bookshop, temporary exhibition room and museum furniture in general;
– Richard PEDUZZI, in partnership with SET FOULQUIER, was commissioned with the layout of the exhibition rooms devoted to the History of the Louvre.
The layout of the third-floor east and south wings of the cour Carrée was designed by Italo ROTA and SETEC FOULQUIER.

## 3. THE CONTRACTORS

The main contractors involved in the completion of the project were [1] :

### Cour Napoléon
#### Underground works

- ALBOUW-HAMART (assembling and dismantling the Le Vau wall)
- BATIBOIS (interior joinerywork)
- BON & NAGA (fire-screens and fire-doors)
- BOSHER GRAVURE (supply and installation of visitor directions components)
- CAMPENON BERNARD (civil engineering, oratorium)
- CAP SOGETI LOGICIEL ( supply of public information system)
- CGCE (furniture)
- CMP (tiling)
- CROISEAU (spiral staircase, guard-rail, temporary exhibition furniture)

---

1. Contractors for main fabric works and finishings whose contracts, on 1 August 1988, exceeded FF1m. For the cour Napoléon and cour Carrée sectors, they have been categorized according to the nature of the works carried out, and listed in alphabetical order.

- DASSAULT (ticket sales and control systems)
- DELATTRE LEVIVIER (trapdoors and emergency exits)
- DELOFFRE (interior partition walls)
- DENNERY (layout of History of the Louvre rooms and staff restaurant)
- DUMEZ (civil engineering)
- DUTEMPLE (mirrors and glazing)
- EI (centralized technical management)
- EI FNAC (audio-visual facilities)
- ERCO (supply of special lighting)
- EURISOL ( suspended ceilings)
- FICHET BAUCHE (strong-room)
- FISCHER ET FILS (flooring)
- FLUIDELEC (compressed-air network)
- FORCLUM (electricity)
- IC LEFORT FRANCHETEAU (air-conditioning and fire protection)
- JEUMONT SCHNEIDER (automatic switchboard)
- LAURENT BOUILLET (steam network)
- MUNIER POLONOWSKI (relief plans of the Louvre)
- NORD FRANCE (sanitary engineering)
- OTIS (escalators)
- PARENGE (masonry)
- PIERREUX DE FRANCE (stone facing)
- PRADEAU MORIN (layout of staff restaurant and kitchen)
- QUILLERY (berlinoise retaining wall, pyramid mock-up)
- QUINETTE INTERNATIONAL (auditorium seating)
- RCS (elevators, service lifts, and platform elevator)
- ROCACHER et ROSSFELDER ( parquet flooring)
- SATELEC (low-voltage networks, telephone)
- SEFI SOCIETEP (berlinoise retaining wall)
- SIMECSOL (boring)
- SOCIETEP (archaeological excavations, general earthmoving works)
- SOFAPO GAUTIER ( metalwork)
- SORT et CHASLE (ceiling plasterwork)
- SPIE STRINDEL (security of persons and property)
- SPR/LECLAIRE (painting)
- TISSERAND (scenic facilities)
- TRANSFLUIDE (waste disposal)
- ZELL (plumbing)

### Pyramid and basins

- CFEM (metal structure and glazing for the pyramids)
- EI VERGER DELPORTE (basins and pumping stations)
- PRADEAU MORIN (civil engineering, basins)
- SAINT GOBAIN (glass)

### Ground level layout

- BOURBON (sculptor)
- CENTRALE DU GRANIT (supply of granite slabs)
- FONDATION COUBERTIN (casting of the Bernini equestrian statue of Louis XIV)
- FONTES DE PARIS (restoration of lamposts)
- MARBRES DU CANDADO (supply of granite paving)
- PRADEAU MORIN (Sully steps)
- SCREG (temporary roads)
- UNIMARBRES (pavingwork)

### Link to the Denon pavilion

- IC (air-conditioning)
- KONE (elevators)
- OTIS (escalators)
- PRADEAU MORIN - CHANTIERS MODERNES (civil engineering, stonework)

## Cour Carrée

### Restoration of roofing, façades, sculptures, masonry, door and window frames

- ERPIMA (masonry and ashlar stonework)
- GALLOZI (roofing work)
- MARTIN (carpentry for site safety arrangements)
- MIEGE BUHLER (roofing for the Assyrians pavilion)
- MPR (masonry and ashlar stonework)
- PAYEUX (masonry)
- PRADEAU MORIN (masonry and ashlar stonework)
- ROUSSEAU (roofing)
- SACHET BRULET (masonry and ashlar stonework)
- SOFIANOS (sculpture, cleaning and restoration)
- TERP (cleaning and masonrywork)
- UNHIR (cleaning and masonrywork)
- ZELL (roofing and leadwork)

### Earthmoving and archaeological crypts

- CAMPENON BERNARD (civil engineering)
- CERBERUS GUIGNARD (fire safety system in crypts)
- CHARPENTIERS DE PARIS (structural steelwork)
- DECORAMA (interior layout)
- LAURENT BOUILLET (temporary heating and fire safety networks)
- LEFORT FRANCHETEAU (air-conditioning and fire safety)
- MENUISERIE DE FLANDRE (joinerywork)
- PRADEAU MORIN (archaeological excavations)
- PRETEUX (high-voltage electricity)
- QUILLERY (civil engineering in the existing fabric)
- SOULIER (elevators)
- VAN MULLEM (metalwork)

### Ground level layout

- PLEVEN GIQUEL (supply of granite paving stones)
- SNPEP (supply of stoneware paving)
- SNTPP (pavingwork)

### Laboratory, delivery areas, internal service route

- DOLBEAU (plumbing and fire protection)
- EI-PSY (GTC)
- FICHET BAUCHE (strong-room)
- GAUTIER (metalwork, joinery)
- GTME (fire safety)
- LA FOURCRIERE DEZELLUS (fire door)
- OTIS (service lift)
- SAUTELEC (electricity)
- SGE TPI (civil engineering)

- SOCIETEP (archaeological excavations, general earthmoving works)
- SOLETANCHE (retaining works)
- THOMAS HARRISON (painting, facing work)
- TUNZINI NESSI (air-conditioning, smoke extraction)
- VITURAT (damp-proofing)

## Lemonnier underpass

- BORIE SAE CHANTIERS MODERNES (civil engineering)
- SNTPP (carriageway)
- UNIMARBRE-MULTIPOSE (stonework)

## Museum of Fashion

- CHARPENTIERS DE PARIS (structural steelwork, guard rails)
- GUINIER (fire and theft detection, scenographic design)
- JULLY (parquet flooring)
- OLIN ( fabric)
- PIERREUX DE FRANCE (stonework and tiling)
- ROUMIGUIER (metalwork, finish hardware)
- SOE STUC ET STAFF (interior decoration)
- VERGER DELPORTE (electricity and telephone)

## Richelieu wing

- BONALDY (roofing)
- CAMPENON BERNARD (civil engineering)
- DUTEMPLE (mirrors, glazing)
- FERBECK VINCENT (metal air-extractor flues)
- HERVE THERMIQUE (air-conditioning)
- LA FOURCRIERE DEZELLUS (metalwork)
- MILLS (installation protective canopy)
- OTIS (escalator)
- PIERREUX DE FRANCE (stone facing)
- PRETEUX (high voltage electricity)
- QUILLERY (sanitary engineering)
- SPIE STRINDEL (security of persons and property)

The project could never have been completed but for the team spirit and the professionalism shown by each of the contractors to whom the client body and the architects wish to express their gratitude.

## 4. THE DIFFICULTIES ENCOUNTERED IN THE EXECUTION OF MAJOR PROJECTS

The most obvious difficulty arises from the strict time-limits within which the project team has to operate; from the very outset, tasks necessarily overlap and operations have to be planned well ahead. All these operations, however, are inevitably inter-linked; as a result, administrative shortcuts have to be adopted throughout the entire design process and building works – despite the constraints thus imposed on all concerned.

Owing to the high degree of quality and complexity involved, major projects are supremely prestigious operations. Given the extremely short execution deadlines, the sheer number of participants involved in the works, and the scale of financial provision, they exceed normal budgetary allocations; all parties concerned – and in particular, the client body – are saddled with a daunting task from start to finish.

The setting up of a public authority such as the *établissement public* provides a means whereby the overall task can be more accurately defined, thanks to the action of a tightly-knit, highly motivated team. However, some time can elapse before operations get into their stride owing to factors such as the relative inexperience of the newly-created team, the diversity of its members, and the necessity to resort to outside assistance.

In the light of such reflections, it is to be hoped that a specific policy may be adopted for the running of future operations of this nature, and that experienced inter-disciplinary teams can be set up to allow a more efficient solution to the problems that client bodies encounter in the execution of major state building projects, notably with a view to providing improved cost management. Costs can vary considerably in the course of such operations; the introduction of a system of *a posteriori* cost control – more attuned to the actual conditions, where real-time decisions have to be taken – would be preferable to the present *a priori* control arrangements that appear ill-suited to deal with such situations.

## PHOTOGRAPHIC CREDITS

*Aubin Imprimeur*

LIGUGÉ, POITIERS

Achevé d'imprimer en mai 1989
N° d'impression P 31361
Dépôt légal, mai 1989
Imprimé en France

Photocomposition : CGP — Photogravure : Actuel-Repro